Overcoming
Violence

Margot Kässmann

Overcoming Violence

The Challenge to the Churches in All Places

Risk
BOOK SERIES

WCC Publications, Geneva

Cover design: Edwin Hassink

ISBN 2-8254-1228-7

© 1998 WCC Publications, World Council of Churches,
150 route de Ferney, 1211 Geneva 2, Switzerland

No. 82 in the Risk Book Series

Printed in Switzerland

Table of Contents

Drawing by Len Munnik

Preface

In his sermon at the launch of the World Council of Churches' Peace to the City campaign in Johannesburg in August 1997, South African Methodist Bishop Mvume Dandala said, "There is nothing romantic about violence." This sentence struck me as pointing to a fundamental change in recent history. Time and again in our century violence has been romanticized in order to win support for it. In 1914 German young men went off to war carrying flowers given to them by young women and a song on their lips. The soldier was the "real man" defending his country. For what, why and against whom most could not really say. It is difficult to imagine today how a whole generation of young French, British, Belgian, Dutch, German, Austrian males could kill one another for some sort of national pride, or how the churches on all sides could bless their weapons. In Europe today Verdun remains a symbol of the senselessness of that war.

Now it seems that a growing majority of people are no longer prepared to accept excuses for violence. Violence has been demystified, and its theological justification is being questioned. In the 1960s and 1970s violence was seen by a considerable number of people – also within the churches – as a legitimate means of overcoming unjust structures. Today we realize that the very same violence which was meant to liberate people is often enslaving them further. Quite a few of those who once took up arms to defend their rights now say: violence is *not* the way. It is only the cradle of more violence. Many of those who earlier supported liberation movements are now asking themselves whether they took the debate about violence seriously enough.

Yet we must be realistic. Violence is still prevalent in the world today. People are suffering worldwide from structural violence, from the many wars that are still being fought, from violence in daily life. European males today may not be killing one another in war, but they still do so in football stadiums – most notably in May 1985, when 40 people were killed and 256 injured before a championship match in Belgium between Liverpool and Turin.[1] The mass media convey

continuous images of the strong as those who defend themselves with violent means. We live in a world where the
image of violence permeates all sectors of life.

Robert McAfee Brown has warned of the permanent dan-
ger "that those in relatively comfortable circumstances will
remain naïvely insensitive to instances of evil that might
demand more vigorous opposition than relatively comfortable circumstances would suggest".[2] So as a German born
after the second world war and living in a "relatively comfortable" situation, I should perhaps hesitate to write about
violence. But this book is not about judgment; it is about
challenge – a common challenge facing churches and Christians everywhere: if there are almost one billion Christians
living in this world, why do we seem to make so little difference in a world of violence and fear? How can churches and
Christians be encouraged to witness to the belief that loving
our neighbour is the basis of our faith, that nonviolence is a
convincing, active approach to the conflicts in life?

In no way does this book attempt to offer a comprehensive approach to the complex issue of violence. In particular,
it does not take up the research and studies of violence by
anthropologists and other social scientists, on which abundant literature is available for those interested. Rather, this
contribution is meant to draw attention to the tremendous
potential of a new initiative of the World Council of
Churches for linking actions by the churches and stimulating
creative theological reflection. It is meant to encourage
churches to bear witness to the fundamental Christian belief
in nonviolence as a creative force in our times.

Insights for this come from ecumenical history, and I will
draw in particular on my own context, the struggle of the
churches in Germany with the question of violence. At the
same time I will try to indicate some of the theological challenges which accompany this programme. Again, this will
not be done in the manner of scientific research; and, as I
have learned in the ecumenical movement that story-telling
is a way of doing theology, each of the ten chapters begins
with a story – without commentary – which highlights one of

the many possible contexts for reflection. The concluding summary at the end of each chapter can be seen as an element of an outline of the challenges of the WCC's Programme to Overcome Violence.

I am convinced that this programme has the potential to engage the ecumenical movement in an enriching spiritual experience, a fruitful theological debate and a creative process of dialogue with other religions, with civil society, with the world at large. Moreover, it could encourage the churches to live up to what they are called to be: peacemakers. It is with gratitude to the ecumenical movement that I agreed to the suggestion of friends to share with a wider audience some of the challenges we see in the Programme to Overcome Violence.

NOTES

[1] An article in *Zivildienst*, Oct. 1996, pp.12ff., describes efforts to work with football supporters to prevent violence in stadiums.
[2] Robert McAfee Brown, *Religion and Violence*, Philadelphia, Westminster, 1987, p.87.

1. Just Another Programme?

When the World Council of Churches' Central Committee was able to meet in South Africa for the first time ever in January 1994, it was a moment of joy and gratitude, a moment of prayer and praise. For many years the apartheid system, with its legal establishment of racial discrimination and inequality, had been on the Council's agenda; and the clear stand taken by the WCC had caused many conflicts, even among and within member churches. Now that system was about to come to an end. During a festive worship in downtown Johannesburg, Methodist Bishop Stanley Mogoba said in his sermon: After the WCC's Programme to Combat Racism has contributed so much to overcoming apartheid, is it not time to create a Programme to Combat Violence?

South Africa – a few months away from the first free elections in April 1994 – gave an example of the violence which threatens the lives of people all over the world. Joy at the approaching end of apartheid was tempered by the bitter reality of the violence from which especially the black communities were suffering – and the fear that this would spread. In their visits to the townships central committee members were confronted with that reality.

We find ourselves in a situation in which violence threatens the very existence of life on this planet. This is linked to structural violence and to weapons of mass destruction, to the demolition of natural resources and to the erosion of human community by violence within. The inseparable connection between justice, peace and integrity of creation that was one of the key insights of the ecumenical movement in the 1980s is thus illuminated by the reality of violence in the 1990s: God's creation as a whole is being destroyed by injustice, war and ecological crisis. The globalization of the economy has brought with it the insight that violence is a global phenomenon. All over the world there are reports of growing acceptance of the use of violence as a means of conflict resolution. The ideology of the necessity of violence has become so influential that even civil groups have sometimes supported the "war for peace" theory (for example in Sri Lanka, as described in chapter 9).

[The German] Jan Philip Reemtsma, himself the victim of a recent hostage-taking, has spoken of the need to find a "civilizational minimum" in the face of the persistent violence which is a central experience of shock in our century: "Our feeling of helplessness at the end of this century is closely linked with the history of violence. The notion of limits to violence has been thoroughly ruined in this century – in wars, civil massacres, in systems of terror of different kinds."[1] Obviously the Nazi genocide is a decisive element in this perception. More than 60 million people were killed during the second world war. The Holocaust eliminated almost the whole Jewish population of Europe; and the lives of minorities who did not fit or could not adjust were destroyed by an unprecedented system of violence.

Other systems followed: the Stalin era in the Soviet Union and Eastern Europe, the Pol Pot regime in Cambodia, military dictatorships in country after country of Latin America – any list seems incomplete. Yet the Nazi period remains as the example without parallel, because of the integration of every part of daily life into the system of terror. It is probably the systematic approach to the use of violence by the state, combined with the use of weapons of mass destruction that do not discriminate between combatants and civilians, which has created our century's apparent sense of helplessness regarding any concept of a limitation of violence.

Walter Wink has written that "violence is the ethos of our times. It is the spirituality of the modern world. It has been accorded the status of a religion, demanding from its devotees an absolute obedience to death."[2] There is a good deal of evidence to support this judgment. On the other hand, there also seems to be a growing awareness that our world desperately needs a counter-ethos that affirms life in order to create livable conditions for generations to come. Thus peace movements, human rights groups and initiatives for mediation and conflict-resolution can be found on every continent.

So far this new awareness is only a glimpse. Even in Europe, where there are many signs of peaceful cooperation among nation-states more than fifty years after the second world war, one must caution against too much enthusiasm, as the recent wars in the former Yugoslavia and in Chechnya have shown. It seems that only a spark is needed to rekindle hatred and war between nations and ethnic groups. The wealth of Europe is still based on the structural violence of its unjust relationships to the countries of the South. And now, with decreasing wealth and increasing unemployment, violence is also rising within Europe itself.

Georges Casalis is said to have remarked during the Algerian war that there is a violence which liberates and a violence which enslaves. There was still some romanticism about violence then. People talked about the criteria for a "just revolution". It is not only the ruling powers but also those striving for a just society who have justified violence. They have sought norms according to which violent resistance to unjust structures might be legitimized. Summarizing this debate, which was prominent in the 1970s, Wink suggests that "a doctrine of just revolution, however stated, would not urge an indiscriminate use of violence under almost any circumstances, but only a discriminate use of violence under certain circumstances".[3] Today we would be inclined to ask: what is "discriminate" use? Who claims the authority to define the circumstances? Will the worst and most long-term effects of violence not inevitably touch the weakest persons in society?

Looking back at the revolutionary movements of the 1970s, we know today that there is absolutely nothing romantic about violence. Nevertheless, popular culture continues to feed the romanticization of violence and war. While this calls for urgent resistance, the churches in their debates too often briefly lament violence and then struggle with how to sanctify it. The popular legitimization of violence is difficult to escape. But the serious contradiction this creates in almost all of us should not deter us from the search for new perspectives.

The quest for what Reemtsma calls a "civilizational minimum" of nonviolence has had several impulses. It could be sensed after the devastating wars of our century. The nuclear threat in the 1970s and 1980s elicited a widespread peace movement in the countries of the North. Now that violence is beginning to be evident in daily life within societies which have been relatively safe since the second world war, new emphasis is being given to the question of how to deal with it. While years of debate about structural violence against the countries of the South have not raised sufficient awareness in the North of the reality of the suffering thus caused, the situation today may well be a *kairos* moment for approaching this issue also in terms of violence and nonviolence.

Violence affects all societies at all levels. There is no island of immunity to violence any more. Any newspaper on any day is full of reports about violence (while nonviolent action scarcely seems to be considered newsworthy – unless it provokes a violent reaction). Take an example from a single day in 1997:[4]

- *Algeria*: The leader of the Armed Islamic Group (GIA) justifies the killing of women and children in order to construct a theocratic Islamic state.
- *Central America*: Ten years after the Esquipulas peace agreement there is no longer any military fighting, but social injustice has brought rising crime rates throughout the region. Youth gangs are spreading. El Salvador has 140 homicides per 100,000 inhabitants per year.
- *Germany*: Seven youths have attacked a 22-year-old asylum-seeker, injuring him severely.
- *Germany*: A study published by Ernst Klee shows that the majority of German doctors in the 1930s and 1940s readily took up the possibilities offered by the Nazis for experiments on human beings.
- *Japan*: An attempt to find agreement among 140 states on the reduction of greenhouse gases in preparation for the Kyoto conference on climate change failed.
- *Kenya*: Despite violent clashes in Mombasa, President Daniel arap Moi rejects calls for reform.
- *Korea*: South Korea dampens hopes for an agreement about peace negotiations with North Korea.

- *The Netherlands*: The UN Tribunal in the Hague rejects as mere propaganda the claim of Radovan Karadzic that his trial for war crimes should be held in the Bosnian Serb republic.
- *Pakistan*: Twelve people are killed and more than forty injured during attacks against mosques by religious fanatics.
- *Palestine*: President Yasser Arafat says that Israeli sanctions against the Palestinians are a declaration of war against the civilian population.

Realities like these, reported in all regions, convinced the members of the WCC Central Committee in 1994 to take up the challenge put to them by Bishop Mogoba. If violence is found all over the world, so are Christian congregations. A programme undertaken by the WCC could enable linking the global and the local. The WCC could serve as a switchboard for experiences and theological reflection. So the Central Committee approved the decision to "establish a Programme to Overcome Violence, with the purpose of challenging and transforming the global culture of violence in the direction of a culture of just peace".[5]

In his original proposal Bishop Mogoba had used the term "combat", by analogy to the Programme to Combat Racism. But this had seemed an inappropriate term in regard to violence, and "overcome" was chosen instead. Later this raised some pointed questions. Is it really possible to *overcome* violence? Has violence not been a fact of human life since Cain and Abel? Has the WCC fallen under an illusion? But on further reflection the term has gained credibility. It can be linked to Paul's words in his letter to the Romans: "Overcome evil with good" (12:21). Paul is talking here about eschatological behaviour which one can practise according to the possibilities of this world.[6]

This may well be applied to the programme before us: let us act according to our possibilities in order to create a sign of the eschatological reality in our world. In this sense "overcoming violence" is a fitting description of where the programme is heading and of the specific challenge posed to the churches.

The challenge of violence has been with Christians since the time of Jesus Christ himself. He died a violent death and was seen by many as a revolutionary leader. Yet he provoked even his friends by urging them to respond to violence with nonviolence (cf. Matt. 26:51f.). As the church became an institution of power, it came to use violent means itself, symbolized in the Crusades, the Inquisition, witch-hunts, colonialism. People of other faiths became the main victims of Christian claims of power. Christian antisemitism found its unprecedented climax in the Holocaust. Today it is between Muslims and Christians that prejudice and tension are growing in many places. The Christian sense of superiority reached a climactic point in the destruction of aboriginal peoples' heritage and faith in the age of colonization – as those whose ancestors were heathens in relation to the Jews used that very term to justify the repression of others.

But the churches were "violent offenders" also among themselves, fighting one another because of their denominational differences. During his visit to France in 1997 Pope John Paul II remembered and lamented the St Bartholomew's Day massacre in 1572, when thousands of Protestants were killed by Roman Catholics in France. Time and again churches have also identified themselves with a political cause, taking sides and becoming part of a violent conflict. While churches have grown together in many ways during this ecumenical century, very few have decisively opted for nonviolence; and while some churches are struggling with this challenge, most churches hardly debate the issue.

Nevertheless, the knowledge of the original call to become peacemakers has stayed alive in the Christian community. Like a red thread this knowledge can be traced in a counter-history of those who have dared to overcome evil with good. The great saints of our century – of different religions and denominations – Gandhi, Martin Luther King, or Mother Teresa – were respected because of their deep commitment to nonviolence. John Kennedy said that either humanity will put an end to war or war will put an end to humanity. In other words, the future belongs to nonviolence or there will be no future.

In rediscovering the call to nonviolence in depth, the church can regain strength and credibility. But this will happen only in so far as the churches themselves and Christians all over the world engage in prayer and in nonviolent action. The idea that nonviolence is passive is a profound misunderstanding. Nonviolence is a very active way of life, a way that needs a great deal of courage and a readiness to face up to one's own fears. In the search for a "civilizational minimum" of nonviolence the churches could play a leading role, provided that they are willing to take a close look at their own history and their own theology. This means a critical re-examination of the grounds on which violence has been legitimized as well as an opening up of the great possibilities offered by the biblical testimony to our discourse on violence and nonviolence. Even in the secular world the question is being asked: Is religious language needed to overcome violence? With its language and methodology of repentance, renewal, peace-making and forgiveness, the Christian faith can contribute to the theory and praxis of nonviolence.

As the churches have something to bring to the worldwide community, they must be part of the civil society which struggles to overcome violence in order to be credible. There is no justification for staying silent. Yet there is a need to confront the church itself with its own history and to ask whether nonviolence has to be declared a mark of the church. In contemporary ecclesiological debates this is highly controversial.

* * *

While it is true on the one hand that violence is the ethos of our times, on the other hand there is a growing awareness that the cycle of violence must be broken in order to protect life. The churches are challenged to take a leading role in proving that nonviolence is an active approach to conflict resolution. Indeed, it is not only one possible way, but the necessary way in order to stop the daily destruction of innocent lives.

NOTES

[1] "Die Skala des Scheusslichen ist nach unten offen", an interview with Jan Philipp Reemtsma in *Frankfurter Rundschau*, 14 Apr. 1997, p.7 (translation by the author).

[2] Walter Wink, *Engaging the Powers*, Minneapolis, Fortress, 1992, p.15.

[3] *Ibid.*, p.58.

[4] All these items are taken from the *Frankfurter Rundschau*, 8 Aug. 1997.

[5] For the full text of the Central Committee decision, see *Programme to Overcome Violence: An Introduction*, Geneva, WCC, 1997, p.17.

[6] Cf. Ernst Käsemann, *An die Römer*, 4th ed., Tübingen, J.C.B. Mohr/Paul Siebeck, 1980, p.337.

2. A Look at the WCC History

The Vancouver assembly of the WCC in 1983 drew the attention of churches around the world to the exploitation of the people of the Pacific islands by the nuclear testing of the dominant nations. Various international signs of solidarity and engagement followed; and the Pacific became for many people a symbol of the interconnectedness of justice, peace and integrity of creation. Nevertheless in the mid-1990s the French government resumed nuclear testing there against the explicit will of the people of the Pacific, the governments which had signed the international treaty against nuclear testing and the peace movement supporting the treaty. After the final test the French left the Pacific without ever seeing the need to consult the Pacific people. During a WCC meeting shortly thereafter a delegate from the Pacific said: "The French are leaving us behind after the testing with hatred deep in our hearts. How can we look for reconciliation, if there is no vis-a-vis?"

The question of the churches' response to violence has been with the WCC since its founding. During the years before the second world war the *Deutsche Christen* ("German Christians") had gone terribly astray. In response to Hitler's accusation that Christianity is a religion for slaves and cowards, they emphasized words like "strength" and "fight", rejected compassion as a sign of effeminacy and called pacifism a destructive (!) phenomenon. At the same time, they declared race and nation as God-given, even calling on the German people to keep their race "pure".[1] When Hitler came to power certain parts of the church cooperated with and even strengthened his ideology. The *Deutsche Christen* legitimized war as well as antisemitism and racism, thus becoming part of the destructive forces that led to the Holocaust and the second world war. Even the Confessing Church – which courageously resisted the Nazis' claims – did not in such a political climate find the strength clearly and openly to resist the persecution of the Jewish population as well as of gypsies, homosexuals, communists and many others.

There were a few exceptions. One of them, Dietrich Bonhoeffer, was clearly influenced by his own ecumenical experiences. Responsibility was the central theme of Bonhoeffer's ethics. In his reflections on the relation of church and state two phases can be distinguished: a first phase of trying to keep off the threat, and a second phase of reflecting in advance on a new beginning after the catastrophe.[2]

While Bonhoeffer himself chose to take part in plans to assassinate Hitler in order to prevent more evil, Robert McAfee Brown writes, he "would never have argued that the decision set a precedent justifying future murders. It remained for him the extreme instance, the exception from which it was not possible to argue to other possible exceptions."[3] The question whether the murder of a tyrant can be legitimized by Christian ethics in order to prevent more atrocities has been with Christians for almost as long as there has been theological reflection. Today it arises in a different way whenever victims of violence call on the international community for armed intervention. Love of the neighbour and the commitment to nonviolence seem to contradict one another in such cases. "But a 'justified' use of violence in one case often sets the stage for a series of justifications of violence. Conflicts 'solved' by force in one generation fester to become the source of later conflicts and even longstanding animosities."[4]

While reflecting on his own decision, Bonhoeffer watched closely the stance of his church. After the assault against Hitler failed, he began to reflect on a possible new course for the German church after the disaster that was obviously coming. He urged W.A. Visser 't Hooft, general secretary of the WCC in process of formation, to encourage the German churches to confess their guilt and to take responsibility for their failure in the Third Reich. After Bonhoeffer's execution and the end of the war, Visser 't Hooft took up that suggestion and sent a delegation of the WCC to the Council of the Evangelical Church in Germany, meeting in Stuttgart in October 1945, with an invitation to join the WCC. This in itself was an astonishing act of reaching out the hand of reconciliation by the members of the delegation, who came from France, Britain, the Netherlands, Switzerland and the USA – countries to which Nazi Germany had brought tremendous suffering and pain.

The confession suggested by Bonhoeffer was finally proclaimed in Stuttgart on 19 October 1945 and made it possible for the German churches to become founding members of the WCC at its first assembly in 1948 in Amsterdam. In the Stuttgart Declaration the Evangelical Churches in Germany accused themselves of not confessing more courageously, praying more faithfully, believing more joyously and loving more fervently. With all its limitations, this may be seen as an example of a church trying to face its own failure to resist violence.

More than 50 years later, delegates to the WCC's world conference on mission and evangelism in Salvador de Bahia, Brazil, assembled on 30 November 1996 at the Solar do Unhao, the ill-famed quay where some six to twelve million Africans, who had been transported like cattle over the ocean, landed and were sold into slavery. The church had been complicit in this violence, and only a few Christians had spoken out against slavery's destruction of human lives. Now, hundreds of years later, it was possible to confess the guilt of the colonial nations involved in the slave trade, of the Africans who assisted by selling their brothers and sisters, and of the churches who remained silent.

In these two situations the call to nonviolence has made its way. Guilt and failure could at least be recognized, if only many years later. The true meaning of the gospel could be heard in a confession of guilt which brought its liberating power to the surface. But how can these insights be carried on so that the call to witness to nonviolence is not just recognized in hindsight? A confession of guilt is useful only if it leads to renewal, so that in a new situation we do not fail again. If we believe it is possible to learn from history, the failure of the church in the past must be a signpost for the present. One possibility for such learning lies in a rediscovery of the power of oral tradition, music and poetry. A good example of how this message can be borne from generation to generation is the song "We Shall Overcome". Rooted in the violent oppression of the era of slavery in the Americas, it was often sung during the civil rights movement led by Martin Luther King, and its hopeful words are heard today in many situations of nonviolent resistance around the world.

The suffering and devastation of the second world war had a great impact on the churches, leading them to reflect on what might be their contribution to a world without war. Pacifism was by no means the only Christian option with regard to war and peace acknowledged at the WCC's Amsterdam assembly; there were two others: the state as a divine order which may oblige Christians to defend their country, and the so-called just war doctrine – the traditional position that a state may be justified under a certain set of conditions in resorting to military force. There was a growing acknowledgment that the use of weapons of mass destruction would make it impossible to fulfill the criteria according to which war could be considered an act of justice. The just war doctrine thus had a very critical function – but it seemed still valid to some.

The delegates to the Amsterdam assembly declared unequivocally that war is contrary to the will of God. But it was not long before this straightforward testimony was put to the test by new wars; and the outbreak of war in Korea in 1950 led to severe strains on the community of churches within the WCC. Nevertheless, many continued to see the ecumenical movement as a peace movement. There was hope that the churches' growing together in unity would reduce the role of religion as a factor of war. This remains until today as a crucial challenge for the ecumenical movement.

The question of violence took a new form in the late 1960s and early 1970s. Confronted with racism and the liberation struggle, many churches entered the debate about a "just revolution". During the WCC's world conference on Church and Society in Geneva in 1966, the voice of the churches from the South could no longer be ignored or dismissed by referring to the traditional concepts of ecumenical social ethics, such as the idea of the "responsible society", for these very approaches were being questioned.

Especially during the section work of the Geneva conference, the possibility that the violence of a revolution could be a lesser evil than the existing structural violence was debated:

> It cannot be said that the only possible position for the Christian is one of absolute nonviolence... The use by Christians of revolutionary methods – by which is meant violent overthrow of an existing political order – cannot be excluded a priori. For in such cases it may very well be that the use of violent methods is the only recourse of those who wish to avoid prolongation of the vast covert violence which the existing order involves.[s5]

It is noteworthy that the "left wing" of the ecumenical movement was here using an argument similar to that often advanced by the "conservatives": that violence must be used only for a "good cause". Whether that cause is revolution or stabilizing the balance between the superpowers or defending human rights or protecting the market occurs almost as a matter of the context and one's convictions about it. The argument for the means is the same.

Historically, it seems that whenever "a violent movement has seized power, it has made violence the law of power";[6] and already at the Geneva conference in 1966 there were warnings to remember the day after the revolution.

It must be pointed out that there is no apparent indication in history of a situation in which genuine peace came out of violence, although the victory of the allied forces over Hitler in the second world war is often cited as such a case. In retrospect, one must first of all assess why it was not possible within Germany itself to prevent the Nazi regime. The reasons usually mentioned by historians include the burdens of the Versailles treaty, the crisis of the Weimar republic and the latent antisemitism; yet former chancellor Willy Brandt has suggested that all this might have been overcome by a "democratic-militant resistance".[7] At the same time some are asking today why, if the victory of the allied forces was too late to save the European Jews, it had to come at so high a price? If we take into account the nuclear bombs on Hiroshima and Nagasaki, the death of tens of thousands of civilians in cities during the last few months, most of all the coming of the Iron Curtain with all its consequences – was this a break in the cycle of violence or just the turning of a new page? In the light of the nonviolent revolution of the East Germans in 1989, it is interesting to ponder on whether at some stage the Germans would have been able to overthrow the Nazi regime and to fight for democracy themselves. Certainly violence in Europe continued after 1945. There was no liberation but new violence, as was proved in the German Democratic Republic in 1953, Hungary in 1956, Czechoslovakia in 1968 and Poland in the 1980s. The war continued as a cold war – and sometimes a hot war, as in Korea, Algeria, Cuba and Vietnam. The cycle of violence was not broken despite the many sincere hopes and despite the many lives sacrificed.

In response to the Geneva conference, the WCC's fourth assembly (Uppsala 1968) asked the Central Committee "to explore means by which the World Council could promote studies on nonviolent methods of achieving social change bearing in mind that the issue of using violent or nonviolent methods of social change has been raised in the reports of some sections".[8] Under the shock of the assassination of Martin Luther King – who had been invited to preach the opening sermon – and inspired by an address by James Baldwin, the Uppsala assembly also initiated a process which led to the establishment of the Programme to Combat Racism (PCR). The unanimous rejection of racism within the ecumenical movement had never been in doubt, but divisions became apparent as soon as the PCR Special Fund was created to support groups and movements fighting against racism in very concrete ways.

The situation was extremely complicated. Those supporting the Council's solidarity with groups and movements struggling against racism at the local level, recognizing that the WCC after having spoken "so long and so massively"[9] just had to act, felt obliged to approve the Special Fund without question. The divide between those who favoured and those who opposed any financial support to liberation movements was so deep that one either belonged to one side or to the other, as veterans of the ecumenical movement report. There seemed to be no room for struggling with the questions, reservations and objections raised about the fact that some of the groups to which the Council gave money were using violence in the fight for freedom. The only consistent answer was the insistence that it was not for weapons but only for humanitarian aid that the money was given.

A detailed historical analysis of this entire period remains to be written; and it is clear that many emotions are involved. Accounts of human rights violations by Southern African liberation movements which have subsequently become the recognized governments in their nations have placed the question of legitimization of violence on the WCC's agenda again.[10] Perhaps the time has come for differentiation, showing how it is possible fully to support the PCR and to deal with the violations of human rights committed by liberation movements at the same time. Moreover, the Programme to Overcome Violence might open a new perspective on the struggle against, for example, the "new racism" spreading in Europe.

To return to the ecumenical debate of the 1970s: the report on "Violence, Nonviolence and Social Change" adopted by the WCC Central Committee in 1973 "reflected a new stage of the ecumenical debate... and revealed a growing reluctance to condemn categorically those groups which felt obliged to use force in attacking entrenched social, racial and economic injustice".[11] The discussion was on the legitimacy of violence: is violence legitimate if it aims at the liberation of people from oppression? Despite what is sometimes claimed, the report of 1973 does not legitimate that violence. But the ecumenical reflection of those days showed a great deal of sympathy within the ecumenical movement for liberation movements. This was a prerequisite for the credibility of a community of churches that was speaking about justice and liberation. It did not however mean an obligation to tolerate violence. It could be said that the means of nonviolent resistance had not been sufficiently developed at that time; moreover, there seems to have been in some quarters a mood of revolution which did not even leave room for such ideas. The Vietnam war, the close linkage of poverty and oppression in the South to rapid development in the North, and the cries for justice being heard everywhere influenced the debate profoundly. In the North as well, so-called "revolutionary" movements like the Red Army Fraction in Germany were taking up arms against what they considered a fascist and unjust state.

While this revolutionary mood still prevailed at the WCC's fifth assembly (Nairobi 1975), the delegates also declared their readiness to live without the protection of weapons, which in turn served as an impulse for many local and regional level groups to make similar declarations. The key factor in changing attitudes in those days was probably the nuclear threat, felt most strongly in the North. While the development debate continued, a new peace movement was in formation. By the end of the 1970s the nuclear threat had become the main focus of the ecumenical debate on violence, sometimes at the risk of making justice issues secondary.

A central event was the WCC's hearing on disarmament held in Amsterdam in November 1981. Its report, *Before It's Too Late*, was received by the Central Committee in 1982 and commended to the churches as "a remarkable aid for study and discussion... and in taking the first steps towards general and complete disarmament". The churches were called "to take a clear position".[12] This was a significant encouragement for peace movements within the churches, though how seriously the member churches of the WCC really took those recommendations varied.

All this set the stage for the WCC's sixth assembly (Vancouver 1983), where the debate on violence and nonviolence became part of the reflections within the conciliar process on Justice, Peace and the Integrity of Creation.

* * *

A longing for the abolition of war and a debate about the possibility of a just revolution – a legitimate use of violence to advance the cause of justice – have historically been the two focal points of the discussion of violence within the ecumenical movement. The Programme to Overcome Violence has a different point of reference, looking at the red thread of nonviolence and nonviolent action, and a much broader perspective, including the violence experienced in daily life. Thus it enters new ground. To discover the power of nonviolence in international conflict, in the struggle for justice and in daily life might free us for new creativity and a fresh look at history. But the ongoing dilemmas must be faced, especially the question of the victims of violence.

NOTES

[1] Cf. "Die Richtlinien vom 6. Juni 1932", in Krumwiede, Greschat, et al., eds, *Kirchen- und Theologiegeschichte in Quellen, Neuzeit*, Part 2, Neukirchen, Neukirchener Verlag, 1980, pp.118f.

[2] See Karl Martin, "Die theologische Wahrnehmung des Problems Staat-Kirche bei Dietrich Bonhoeffer", *Hessisches Pfarrerblatt*, no.6, 1997, pp.196ff.

[3] Brown, *Religion and Violence*, p.88.

[4] Paul N. Anderson, "Jesus and Peace", in Marlin E. Miller and Barbara Nelson Gingerich, eds, *The Church's Peace Witness*, Grand Rapids, Eerdmans, 1994, p.124.

[5] *World Conference on Church and Society*, Geneva, WCC, 1966, p.143.

[6] Jacques Ellul, *Violence: Reflections from a Christian Perspective*, New York, Seabury, 1969, p.101.

[7] On this see "Willy Brandt und der unglückliche Zerfallsprozess", *Frankfurter Rundschau*, 29 Dec. 1997, p.13.

[8] Cited in "Violence, Nonviolence and Social Change", in *Violence, Nonviolence and Civil Conflict*, Geneva, WCC, 1983, p.10.

[9] Ernst Lange, *Die ökumenische Utopie*, Stuttgart, Kreuz Verlag, 1972, p.129.

[10] An example is the tensions surrounding the publication of *Namibia: Breaking the Wall of Silence*, by Siegfried Groth; cf. *idea*, nos 40-41, 1 Apr. 1996.

[11] *Loc. cit.*, p.11.

[12] Paul Abrecht and Ninan Koshy, eds., *Before It's Too Late*, Geneva, WCC, 1983, p.ix.

3. Nonviolence and the "Conciliar Process"

In the former German Democratic Republic, the Old Testament prophet Micah became a threat to the state. Anyone who wore a small badge with the words "Swords to Ploughshares" (Micah 4:3) and a corresponding symbol was at risk, since this was forbidden. During the 1983 German Protestant Kirchentag, whose theme was "Dare trust – dare peace", a peace group took the liberty of forging an actual sword into a ploughshare. Several thousand people sang and prayed during the 90 minutes the smith needed for his task. This was a deeply meaningful ceremony for the peace movement in the GDR, encouraging many people there to carry on the struggle to create peace using the means of peace. Here was an early step on the way to the nonviolent revolution of 1989 which led to the tearing down of the Berlin wall, the best-known symbol of the Iron Curtain.[1]

Within the WCC the conciliar process for Justice, Peace and Integrity of Creation (JPIC) can be seen as the immediate predecessor of the Programme to Overcome Violence. The learning process of the former flowed into the creation of the latter. Insights gained in the areas of theology and campaigning led to new creativity.

The delegation of the Protestant churches in the German Democratic Republic put in motion the call for a council for peace before the Vancouver assembly in 1983. They recalled the appeal of Dietrich Bonhoeffer at an ecumenical gathering in Fanö, Denmark, in 1934 for a "great ecumenical council of the holy church of Christ" to address the militarization of that era in order "to take the weapons out of the hands of her sons in the name of Christ and to forbid war and to pronounce God's peace to the raging world".

The Vancouver appeal grew out of a process within the GDR to resist the accelerated militarization at the front-lines of the cold war. In both Germanys the stationing of cruise missiles had given birth to an unprecedented peace movement. The church was challenged to give testimony to the call to nonviolence. Conscientious objection was declared the more faithful witness; not only the use but also the production and deployment of nuclear weapons were declared a sin against humanity. These affirmations by the Christian peace movement created an intense debate within the churches. When the legitimacy of military chaplains and the Christian faith of members of the army were questioned in West Germany, it produced a tension within the Christian community that was not easy to bear.

In the debates and discussions in Vancouver the forthright affirmations of the Christian peace movements in Germany and elsewhere underwent a necessary process of ecumenical learning. The result was the conviction that justice, peace and the integrity of creation belong together: one cannot gain one at the cost of losing the others. In the end the assembly called on the WCC "to engage member churches in a conciliar process of mutual commitment (covenant) to justice, peace and the integrity of creation". The years after Vancouver saw various attempts to take up this challenge by way of regional meetings, WCC-initiated conferences and finally a world convocation on JPIC in Seoul in 1990.

At Seoul the gap between the perceptions of contextual challenges arising in different places around the world where people feel the threats to justice, peace and creation in daily life and the search for widely accepted ecumenical convictions proved too wide to bridge in a common statement. Nevertheless, ten affirmations were adopted and four main covenants celebrated.[2] Regarding violence and nonviolence the Seoul documents saw a concretization of the act of covenanting for JPIC in the commitment to "a culture of active nonviolence which is life-promoting and is not a withdrawal from situations of violence and oppression but is a way to work for justice and liberation". Seoul called for "a global nonviolent service which can advance the struggle for human rights and liberation and serve in situations of conflict, crisis and violence." And Affirmation VI of the Seoul document reads:

> We *affirm* the full meaning of God's peace. We are called to seek every possible means of establishing justice, achieving peace and solving conflicts by active non-violence... We *commit* ourselves to practise nonviolence in all our personal rela-

tionships, to work for the banning of war as a legally recognized means of resolving conflicts and to press governments for the establishment of an international legal order of peacemaking.[3]

While the peace debate at that time still focused on armed conflict and especially the nuclear threat, linking it to the justice debate contributed an important additional insight: the recognition that the question of structural violence and the reality of violence in poverty-stricken regions and ghettos are two parts of one and the same picture. At the same time, the realization of the interconnectedness of justice and peace with the integrity of creation helped to show how injustice is a condition of permanent structural and economic violence and to place ecological destruction in the category of violence. In hindsight, violence emerges as the linking term expressing the threat against justice, peace and creation.

In 1991 the WCC held its seventh assembly in Canberra. The development of the conciliar process for JPIC was certainly high on the agenda; yet a more immediate factor dominated many of the discussions: the assembly was meeting during the Gulf war, and news about air attacks against Iraq were part of the daily reality. While many delegates criticized their governments, they also knew that an overwhelming percentage of the population in many of their countries were in favour of those attacks. During a special hearing it became clear that, while all agreed that the conflict had no religious basis as some had claimed, those delegates arguing for an unconditional ethics of peace and those justifying the military action to reverse the Iraqi invasion of Kuwait had difficulty finding common ground. Again the WCC was faced with the question: can war be legitimized as a last resort to end oppression? While it had seemed that the conciliar process had found consensus in a negative answer, now the just war theory again played a role in the argument.

On the last day of the assembly the final version of a statement on the Gulf war was put before the delegates. While it confirmed the Amsterdam declaration that war is contrary to the will of God and that there is in principle no just war in times of the existence of weapons of mass destruction, the gap between those arguing for peace without compromise and those justifying the use of violence against those breaking peace seemed to widen. Konrad Raiser, then a delegate of the Evangelical Church in Germany, proposed integrating into the text a sentence rejecting any theological or moral justification by the churches of the use of military force, using language already accepted in Seoul. This was at first agreed, but when it seemed subsequently that it would threaten the acceptance of the document as a whole, a second vote was taken and it was deleted. This episode is a good indication of the tensions the Canberra assembly had to face. The statement as finally adopted included a call to end the war, while it did not explicitly condemn the military attack against Iraq.

Several lessons were learned in this process: that justice and peace are inseparable, that violence is a threat to life in many forms, and that the dilemmas and tensions over how to respond to violence are not only out there in the world but within the churches themselves. The Canberra assembly might have affirmed as a conviction of the WCC that there is no theological legitimization for violence if it had not been for the profound emotions elicited by the Gulf war. The conviction was still not deep enough; the different approaches which were side by side in Amsterdam in 1948 still existed.

The Canberra discussion of the Gulf war made it necessary to postpone the wider debate on nonviolence. During the years that followed, the changes in Eastern Europe, the wars in the former Yugoslavia and Rwanda, and discussions of intervention and economic sanctions occupied the Council. Again the churches had no clear voice – and in some cases were proving to be part of the problem. In Johannesburg in 1994, as we have seen, the discussion of violence was explicitly taken up again by the WCC. The rejection of any theological legitimization of violence is still on the agenda, and the insights gained may finally enable the ecumenical movement to arrive at a consensus. One thing has clearly been learned: any time there is a violent conflict in which innocent lives are destroyed, deep emotions are stirred up, and Christians will once again be faced with the dilemma of how to put an end to killing and to human rights violations. It is high time for the churches to gain experience with nonviolent means in order not to be limited to old methods which have proved to be no solution.

The ecumenical movement resumes its discourse on violence and nonviolence in a world that has changed. Today, except for acute situations like the recent nuclear tests in India and Pakistan, it is the daily violence and the resulting sense of insecurity in everyday life which are more likely to be on people's minds than the issue of the legitimacy of the use of violence in civil conflicts or action for social change. While the poor still suffer the most, violence also has reached the rich within societies. While the countries of the South are still the main victims of structural violence, it is spreading in the North as well. All this suggests a *kairos* moment for the churches together to take up the debate again in a new context.

* * *

The WCC's conciliar process for justice, peace and creation (JPIC) was an important step on the way to the decision to establish a Programme to Overcome Violence, since violence is a threat to all three elements. Insights gained in the JPIC process regarding structural violence, economy and ecology can be used to conceptualize and shape new ecumenical approaches, which will have to challenge any legitimization of violence by churches. There is hope that one day the churches will not be part of the problem but a significant factor in overcoming violence. If the churches themselves only lament violence but do not dare actively to engage in nonviolence, they are betraying that hope.

24

NOTES

[1] Cf. Friedrich Schorlemmer, *Die Wende in Wittenberg*, Wittenberg, 1997, pp.21ff.
[2] For reflections on the process leading to Seoul and the convocation itself, see D. Preman Niles, ed., *Between the Flood and the Rainbow*, Geneva, WCC, 1992.
[3] The passages from Seoul cited here are from *Now Is The Time: Final Document and Other Texts*, Geneva, WCC, 1990, pp.29, 27, 17.

4. Violence and Nonviolence in the Bible

Meeting at the monastery of Kykkos, Cyprus, in 1997, the WCC Executive Committee adopted a statement on the situation in that divided country. It strongly disapproved the 1974 invasion of Cyprus by Turkish military forces, deplored the recent acts of violence along the buffer zone and re-affirmed the Council's support for a comprehensive negotiated settlement of the Cyprus conflict. Other WCC member churches were urged to encourage and accompany the Church of Cyprus as it seeks to be faithful to Jesus Christ, the Prince of Peace. One morning during worship in the ancient chapel of the monastery, Psalm 3 was read: "Rise up, O Lord! Deliver me, O my God! For you strike all my enemies on the cheek; you break the teeth of the wicked." A number of Executive Committee members remarked on the deep contradiction they sensed between that description of a violent God and the statement on Cyprus which they had just approved.

Many Christians have struggled with the dilemma of biblical passages that refer to or appeal for violent action by God. The violent God and violence by God's people is hardly an isolated theme in the Hebrew part of the Bible. One scholar reckons that the Old Testament contains 600 passages of explicit violence, 1000 verses attributing violent action to God – both stories of God ordering killing and of God killing others.[1] Yahweh is described as a warrior (Ex. 15:3), the Lord uses weapons (Hab. 3:9,11-12), God even fights actively *against* the chosen people (Lam. 2:5). It is not easy to deal with this heritage. Some have argued that this language is just a pointer to God's being involved in rather than aloof from history, that in engaging in real conflict God works out the divine purposes.[2] Others clearly object: "Are we to say that with God the end justifies the means, when we know it does not work that way among human beings?"[3]

In recent years considerable attention has been devoted to the thesis of René Girard that violence in the Bible is necessary to unmask sacred violence as a lie. His argument that a nonviolent God uses violence in order to expose it and thus to reveal the nonviolent nature of the divine is certainly very enlightening and appealing, if rather complex. It underlines the challenge for Christianity to witness truly to the overcoming of the mechanisms of violence, as Jesus did.[4] But one must also be cautious here about making too strong a separation between the Old Testament and the New Testament. If the New Testament is seen as revealing a "better religion", the first part of the Bible might easily be downgraded as a secondary revelation or even abolished from the Christian faith in the manner of the ancient Marcionite heresy. This points to the importance of taking up in interreligious dialogue, particularly among Christians, Jews and Muslims, the whole question of violence.

In fact there is ambiguity regarding the legitimization of violence within the Hebrew part of the Bible. Partly this is due to the differences in context and perceptions among the authors. Certainly the longing for a God who fights for the people and the understanding of crisis as a punishment from God are well known in almost all religions and all contexts, including Christianity. Soldiers wear "God with us" on their belts and revolutionaries arouse support with slogans like "God is with the people".

But alongside the clear references to a warrior God, a red thread of nonviolence runs through the Old Testament. This seems to be the much more exciting part because it is unusual and unfamiliar. Rather than being troubled or repelled time and again by the legitimization of violence within the Hebrew part of the Bible, we should point to texts like the story of Shiphrah and Puah, an account of courageous civil disobedience – to put it in contemporary terms (Ex. 1:15-22). Or take Isaiah 53 as an example, the well-known passage about the suffering servant from whom others hide their faces as the one pouring out himself to death. We can think of Micah 4:2-4, where swords become ploughshares – or many other visionary texts of the prophets. God gives shalom and God liberates. God leads the Israelites out of Egypt, out of an existence in oppression and violence. There is violence, but God does not stay content with that situation. God gives the strength and creativity to break the chains of oppression nonviolently. God is truly liberating.

There is plenty of evidence within the Hebrew part of the Bible describing God as the giver of shalom. Peace is given to people and to creation; the prophets became the champions of shalom. The Programme to Overcome Violence could give new emphasis to such texts. Much remains to be discovered, and just as feminist theology provided new insights for our reading of scripture, so too might the search for the red thread of nonviolence.

The message of the New Testament is very clear: in his Sermon on the Mount Jesus opens a whole new set of categories. It is not the warriors, the heroes and freedom fighters, the strong and the brave who are blessed, but the poor in spirit, those who mourn, the meek and those who hunger and thirst for righteousness, the merciful, the pure in heart, the peacemakers and the persecuted ones. What a contradiction to the reality of this world!

Often the Sermon on the Mount has been dismissed as an unrealistic, romantic text which is basically of no use in a world of fighting, power and fear. Former West German Chancellor Helmut Schmidt once stated that one cannot do politics with the Sermon on the Mount. Jesus' words about retaliation (Matt. 5:38ff.; Luke 6:29ff.) have been cited often as proof of the inadequacy of the gospel as a guide for living in the real world: "It has seemed impractical, masochistic, suicidal – an invitation to bullies and spouse-batterers to wipe up the floor with their supine Christian victims."[5] Yet there is probably no other New Testament passage that puts such a challenge to reality as it is and gives so much hope that things might be different in this world and will be different in God's future.

Walter Wink has made a brilliant and important differentiation between nonresistance and nonviolence. If we look carefully, he says, we discover that the "turning the other cheek" is an act of humiliating the aggressor, that giving the undergarment is an act of unmasking cruelty, that "going a second mile" is a possible way of protest.[6] Thus we can see

Jesus creatively using the methods of nonviolent resistance to defy the powers and to restore community. The fascinating discovery is that the call in the Sermon on the Mount is to nonviolence, but not to nonresistance. Jesus himself walked the path of nonviolent resistance to the very end. He remained a provocation to the powers even when he was dying on the cross. By his death it became obvious that he was not defeated but continued to be a scandal to the forces of violence.

Nevertheless, there are some passages in the New Testament also which have been regularly used to legitimize violence. One is the story of Jesus cleansing the temple (Matt. 21:12ff.; Mark 11:15ff.). Jesus drives out of the temple those who are buying and selling, overturning tables and chairs in the process, even using a whip according to the related account in the gospel of John (2:13-16). Several explanations have been given, for instance, that this should be interpreted as a prophetic action.[7] But if Jesus was truly human, we could also assume that his anger on this occasion overtook his conviction that nonviolence is the way. It is obvious that the resort to violence is often an act of weakness, an inability to act otherwise because emotion rules. Why should it be impossible to see Jesus in such a way – angry at seeing the temple misused for economic interests, furious to the point of losing his temper? If the Council of Chalcedon in 451 stated that Jesus was at once truly human and truly divine, we may well see the weaknesses of human beings in him without losing sight of his divine character.

Another passage often used against a pacifist approach is Matthew 10:34ff.: "I have not come to bring peace but a sword." Some declare that Jesus is speaking here not about human beings, but about the powers.[8] If one looks at the verse in the context of the warnings Jesus gives about the hostile reception the disciples will receive (see also Luke 12:51 – not peace but division), it seems rather to be a preparation for the reality that the gospel and those who proclaim it will be rejected: "This promise connotes the martyr, not the murderer."[9]

Later, in the garden of Gethsemane Jesus clearly says to one of his disciples who resists the arrest: "Put your sword back into its place; for all who take the sword will perish by the sword" (Matt. 26:52). This shows that Jesus is very much aware of the cycle of violence. He knows about the reality of powers, of violence. For Christians, however, a different logic prevails, for the one who wants to be great should be the servant of the other (Matt. 20:25). Jesus' teaching as a whole cannot be questioned by single verses like Luke 22:36 ("the one who has no sword must sell his cloak and buy one"). Rather, we see a concept that challenges the "normality" of violence as it is widely accepted. Jesus often provoked even his disciples – when he ate with the publican, listened to the children and loved the one who betrayed him. By his life and by the stories he told, he taught an ethic that considers all involved. Relating this to conflict implies considering the motive and the outcome for all parties involved. A mediation approach to conflict resolution works in precisely the same way.

Nobody knows beforehand whether he or she will in fact have the strength to resist the use of violent means in critical circumstances. Thus there is a need for deep humility on the part of those who advocate nonviolence. It is not for Christians to condemn one who uses violence to defend the human rights of his or her people or family or self. But the teaching of Jesus will always stand in a sharp contradiction to that. Jesus identified with the poor and the weak, but he did not use violence to defend either himself or them. He himself was killed by violence, under the law of a military regime. Even taking into account the few passages where Jesus seems to legitimize violence, we "cannot make Jesus a guerilla fighter, a rebel, a political agitator and revolutionary or turn his message of God's kingdom into a programme of politico-social action, unless we distort and reinterpret all the gospel accounts."[10]

Jesus clearly calls for a peace ethics, for the love of the enemy as well as the friend (John 15:13). The context here shows that this refers to sacrificial love, not to killing someone else for the sake of a friend. Jesus encourages us to dare to walk the path of nonviolence. Wink suggests that he taught a third way, between violence and nonviolence, as a methodology of resistance against the powers of oppression.

With regard to the Hebrew tradition we must choose between two traditions, two images of God. Jesus made that choice for us when on the one hand he did not dissolve the ambiguity between the wrath and the love of God, but on the other hand clearly advised his followers to love their enemies and pray for those who persecute them (Matt. 6:44f.). The peacemakers are called the children of God (Matt. 5:9). "The war that is open to Jesus' followers... is 'reverse fighting', the acceptance of injustice done to oneself, of pain and suffering and even death."[11] On this basis the rejection of violence – not the condemnation of people using violence – should be the univocal contribution of the churches.

* * *

Alongside the tradition of God as a warrior, a red thread of nonviolent action runs through the Old Testament. The WCC's Programme to Overcome Violence provides an occasion for an ecumenical rediscovery of this. Jesus' call to nonviolence cannot be questioned. There is no legitimization of violence for Christians drawing on biblical sources.

NOTES

[1] Cf. Raymond Schwager, *Must There Be Scapegoats?*, San Francisco, Harper & Row, 1987, pp.46f.
[2] Cf. G. Ernest Wright, *The Old Testament and Theology*, New York, Harper & Row, 1969.
[3] Albert Curry Winn, *Ain't Gonna Study War No More*, Louisville, Westminster-John Knox, 1993, p.65.
[4] Cf. René Girard, *The Scapegoat*, Baltimore, Johns Hopkins U.P., 1986, pp.100ff.; and *Violence and the Sacred*, Baltimore, Johns Hopkins U.P., 1977.
[5] Walter Wink, *Engaging the Powers*, p.175.
[6] *Ibid.*, pp.175ff.

[7] Cf. Anderson, "Jesus and Peace", *loc. cit.*, p.120; Winn, *op. cit.*, pp.15f.

[8] Ellul, *Violence*, p.161.

[9] Thus Anderson, *loc. cit.*, p.121.

[10] Hans Küng, *On Being a Christian*, Garden City NY, Doubleday, 1964, p.187.

[11] Winn, *op. cit.*, p.146.

5. Ecclesiological Insights

In December 1992 a delegation from the World Council of Churches travelled to Croatia to visit Bosnian women in refugee camps. The purpose was to find out whether news reports that rape was being used as a weapon of war were rumour or reality. When the delegation subsequently reported having heard and seen proof that the allegations were true, many in the churches were shocked. At the same time – and over the next several years – the WCC was struggling with the question how to deal with this conflict, in which religion had become a rallying point for Roman Catholic Croats, Orthodox Serbians and Muslim Bosnians. Certainly religion was not the basis of the conflict, but instead of being a reconciling factor it served to inflame it. Many were critical of the Council for its own inability to address the matter clearly with its largest member church in the former Yugoslavia. In this context an attempt was made in the WCC Central Committee to note that member churches have a responsibility to speak out boldly against the use of violence and gross violations of human rights committed in the name of their own nation or ethnic group. Not to do so would call into question the commitment of the WCC as a whole to nonviolence, and its credibility as an agent for peaceful resolution of conflicts.[1] This challenge was to become part of the Programme to Overcome Violence.

It is impossible to discuss the challenge of violence and faithful Christian witness without talking about the church. In chapter 1 we pointed to a number of situations in which the church failed to be a witness of Jesus. Too often the longing for power leads churches into temptation. It is not easy to face up to the reality of the bloodshed that has taken place in the name of the church. People were tortured to death in the name of the Lord, political ends were pursued through holy wars, nations were destroyed in order to follow the "great commission" to make disciples of all nations. The good news thus became bad news for many. Realism obliges us in the face of these facts to ask whether there is a defect in the very basis of the church. What do we teach about the church? And what do we learn about it from seeing how it has acted in history?

In recent years the World Council of Churches has followed up one of the questions raised by the conciliar process for JPIC through study and consultation about ecclesiology and ethics. Here we may find some key insights into our questions. If ethics is recognized as an integral part of ecclesiology and not secondary, if the being of the church and the conduct of the church belong together, we might find a clue to the challenge of nonviolence.[2]

While different approaches have been taken to this issue, the intention to link ecclesiology and ethics is not new. There is for instance the search for the *notae ecclesiae* or "marks of the church". While Roman Catholicism, following the Nicene Creed, has identified unity, holiness, catholicity and apostolicity as the marks of the church, the Reformation saw these as attributes; and the Augsburg Confession, for example, declares (Art. VII) that word and sacrament are the key marks. The ecumenical debate about this proceeds from an explication of the ethical dimension within the attributes by way of an acknowledgment of unity, holiness, catholicity and apostolicity as marks that can be actualized within the ecumenical context to a combination of the four marks with the two marks named by the Reformation.[3] This debate is an effort to find ways of integrating ethical convictions into the definition of the church.

Recent studies have shown that Luther already added to the central marks of word and sacrament in order to show how the gospel in life and practice finds its realization in the true church in differentiation from the false church.[4] While many theologians today agree that these additional marks do change in relation to the context in which a church lives, a dilemma remains as to who may define which marks may be added with regard to the changing context.[5] Johannes Dantine suggests that agreement about the marks should be found in any given situation by a "qualitative consensus" which must be reached by the process of formation necessary to differentiate between orthodoxy and heresy.[6] Taking this into account, one possibility today is to add nonviolence as a mark of the true church.

On the other hand, we may also recall the 16th-century definition of the church as *congregatio sanctorum in qua evangelium pure docetur et recte administrantur sacramenta* – the assembly of saints in which the gospel is taught truly and the sacraments are rightly administered. This could become the common point of reference in the ecumenical dialogue for rooting nonviolence in the *esse* or being of the church, because all three major traditions of Christianity – Orthodoxy, Roman Catholicism and Reformation – can see gospel and sacrament as fundamental to the church. As we have seen, nonviolence is at the centre of the gospel.

If we take the *congregatio sanctorum* seriously, we see the community of saints not only as standing before God but also as being a genuine community or *koinonia*. Christians are baptized into this worldwide community. The eucharist is the occasion on which this *koinonia* participates in the sacred elements and becomes a true community of holy people. If this community is following Christ, one of its marks has to be nonviolence. Bread and wine may strengthen them to overcome their fear and to dare nonviolence. Their living together may become an encouragement to live together non-violently. Their failure, their falling back into old ways of violence can be brought to the table of community and before God. Repentance and a new beginning are possible. The aspect of *koinonia* or community – over against an individu-alistic approach – becomes central here. Nonviolence is cer-tainly part of the "eucharistic life-style" which the WCC's Vancouver assembly talked about in 1983.

While the marks of the church would seem to be a con-vincing entry point for anchoring nonviolence in ecclesiol-ogy, there may also be others. One is the Orthodox idea of the liturgy after the liturgy. The experience of equality and community in the eucharistic liturgy is to be continued in daily life. Here we have no separate ethics; rather, ethics is part of the eucharistic celebration and thus part of the being of the church.[7]

Another approach is through the idea of the church as a "confessional" body. In relation to both apartheid and nuclear weapons, the Lutheran churches called for a process which moved from the recognition of a situation as relating to matters of confession to a process of debate that would culminate in declaring a *status confessionis* which might lead to a division of the church. While the relation to the context is evident in this context, there are some difficulties in applying this approach ecumenically. On the one hand, this understanding of confession is not as present in other traditions as among Lutherans; on the other hand, some have judged this approach to be rather abstract and very exclusive.

The church as a "sign of the kingdom" was present in the discussions at the fourth assembly of the WCC (Uppsala 1968) as well as in the Second Vatican Council (1962-65). Here ethics and ecclesiology are linked in the primacy of God's action which aims at a transformation of society and begins in the transformation of the church. The element of the participation of the people of God, of the community, in this struggle for the true church is fundamental. The problematic element in this approach is the temptation to identify God's kingdom too much with the visible church. Such triumphalism is too often contradicted by evidences of the church's failure, out of human incompetence, to be a sign of God's kingdom.

Finally, we should mention briefly the understanding of the church as a sacrament. Sacramental ecclesiology has been present, especially within Roman Catholic reflection but also in Orthodoxy, for many years; and it has become a key element again since the Second Vatican Council. The church is seen as a sign as well as an instrument, the gift of Christ in which the grace of God can be seen.

Whatever the ecclesiological entry point, there is a clear need to link the challenge of nonviolence with reflection about the church. The credibility of Christians today will be measured in relation to their churches. It is time that not only individual Christians but also the churches themselves give witness to the legacy and power of nonviolence. In the perception of people the link between ecclesiology and ethics seems to be much more present than among theologians.

Drawing on the Latin American debate of the 1970s, the Programme to Overcome Violence might once again take up the notion of "ecclesiogenesis". There is an emerging *ecclesia* locally. People concerned about and threatened by violence are coming together at the local level for prayer and worship. There is ecumenism in action, interfaith dialogue in practice. People are working to protect God's creation and to form an *ecclesia* apart from cultural borders. This *ecclesia* is drawing on the people's capacity to overcome violence and rediscovering traditional methods, for example in indigenous contexts. What we find here within the nonviolence movement is also an empowering of the people: they are the church, they set the pace. What the reflection in Latin America concluded about structural and economic violence can also be applied to the phenomenon of violence as a whole: there are no solutions "from above". The people will take their life into their own hands. They will work for a more just and nonviolent society because they are part of the history of God with the people, because they dare to walk in the footsteps of Jesus Christ.

This approach should be linked with the insights of the WCC's third assembly (New Delhi 1961), when the Council talked about the church "in all places", thus beginning on the one hand to take the local context seriously, and on the other hand to connect the many contexts to one ecumenical whole. The one becomes part of the one – a contradiction that brings a reality into view. What great possibilities the ecumenical movement has truly to become a peace movement, to contribute to a world longing for peace and for the nonviolence that nurtures life! Christians live in all countries of the world. They are taught that the other is their brother or sister no matter what ethnic group, what nationality or culture he or she belongs to. If Christians would live according to that knowledge, if churches would proclaim that reality, they would give a convincing example. If more than 53 million Christians in Germany would witness to that, foreigners could no longer be seen as "intruders" or a threat – many of them in fact are Christians, and all of them are the strangers and neighbours we are called to love.

When we discuss ecclesiology in connection with non-violence in the ecumenical context, seeking clarification of what the church is and is meant to be, we must also ask why the so-called Historic Peace Churches – Mennonites, Hut-terites, Quakers, Brethren – have made a clear option for nonviolence while other churches have found it possible to legitimize violence in one way or another. Peace churches have regarded pacifism and nonviolence as a defining mark of the true church; this was part of their reason for breaking with the churches they grew out of. Common to all peace churches is a clear rootedness in scripture and an attempt to see the primitive church as a model. The Quakers, for exam-ple, highlight three objections to war and violence:

> War is not a method appropriate for achieving peace. One's en-emies may be convinced that their cause is just; killing them is not consistent with respect for their conscience and we are not obligated to heed our leaders' call to arms when we know little of the reasons for the war or whose cause is right.[s8]

Separation from the mainline churches happened when-ever the question of war was debated – just as the just war theory developed as soon as Christianity became part of the ruling power. Most mainline churches have tried to find forms of compromise, whether by differentiating violence and force or by developing a theory of just war or by other lines of reasoning. The key difference seems to lie in the def-inition of the relation between church and state. Today sev-eral of the Historic Peace Churches are a well-accepted parts of the ecumenical movement, but their challenge to the other churches seems rarely to be at the centre of debate.

What we can say is that in their hermeneutics these churches have kept a clearer memory and view of the teach-ings of Jesus than the mainline churches, which have far too often accepted so-called realistic views and left witnessing to the gospel's call for peace to a few individuals. Today all churches together know in principle that it is time to witness in common to that call to peace. The Historic Peace Churches, with their longstanding experience, can be of great help ecumenically in finding a way towards a common witness of all churches for peace.

* * *

The Programme to Overcome Violence must elaborate the conviction that nonviolence is rooted in the definition of the church itself. The elementary marks of the church, word and sacrament, may be a meaningful possibility. At the same time, the definition of the church must be discussed: if the POV talks about the daily life of the people and wishes to make visible the emerging movement of nonviolent resistance, it must take into account the fact that at the local level itself the church is emerging. The Historic Peace Churches may be of help in pointing towards that which the world today needs from all churches together: a clear witness to peace and nonviolence. This is a tremendous challenge and possibility, perhaps a kairos *moment for the ecumenical movement to become a decisive contributor to peace – as it was meant to be.*

NOTES

[1] *Minutes of the 44th Meeting of the Central Committee*, Geneva, WCC, 1992, p.64.
[2] Reports from the WCC study and explanatory essays are collected in Thomas F. Best and Martin Robra, eds, *Ecclesiology and Ethics: Ecumenical Ethical Engagement, Moral Formation and the Nature of the Church*, Geneva, WCC, 1997; other helpful material can be found in N. Barney Pityana and Charles Villa-Vicencio, eds, *Being the Church in South Africa Today*, Johannesburg, South African Council of Churches, 1995.
[3] See Margot Kaessmann, *Die eucharistische Vision*, Munich, Kaiser-Grünewald, 1992, pp.313ff.
[4] Cf. *The Identity of the Church and its Service to the Whole Human Being*, vols. 1 and 2, Geneva, Lutheran World Federation, 1977.

[5] Cf. Peter Steinacker, *Die Kennzeichen der Kirche*, Berlin, Vandenhoeck and Ruprecht, 1982, pp.7,9.

[6] Johannes Dantine, *Die Kirche vor der Frage nach ihrer Wahrheit*, Göttingen, Vandenhoeck and Ruprecht, 1980, pp.157ff.

[7] On this see Ion Bria, *The Liturgy After the Liturgy: Mission and Witness from an Orthodox Perspective*, Geneva, WCC, 1996.

[8] Donald F. Durnbaugh and Charles W. Brockwell Jr, "The Historic Peace Churches: From Sectarian Origins to Ecumenical Witness", in Miller and Gingerich, *The Church's Peace Witness*, p.189.

6. Further Challenges for Theological Reflection

In May 1992 during a funeral at the Morning Star Baptist Church in Boston there was a gang-related shooting in the streets. The victim staggered into the church, where he died. The incident made the clergy of the community realize, "If we fail to bring the gospel to the street, the street will bring its message to the church." Consequently, they came together to form the Ten-Point Coalition in order to mobilize the Christian community to start a street ministry based in the local church. A special focus is ministry to the African American and Latino youth who are most at risk from violence. A recent drop in juvenile deaths and related crimes reported in Boston can in part be attributed to the work of the Ten-Point clergy.

The Programme to Overcome Violence will have to confront the tradition of theological thinking about violence beyond the questions of biblical interpretation and ecclesiology that we have looked at in the preceding two chapters. Obviously it is impossible to deal thoroughly with the issues at stake in the scope of a brief chapter, but we can at least enumerate some of them here as a way of pointing to the directions which a theological debate by people from different denominations and contexts might take.

The Christian tradition has rich and deep resources that might give guidance out of many of the dead ends violence leads into. Yet most theologians, apparently in the interest of being "realistic", declare that there is no theological problem of violence and nonviolence because there will always be violence. What theology must discuss are the proportion and the means of violence in relation to its aims. It is taken for granted that it is necessary to overcome violence by violence.[1] But it is equally realistic to observe that violence never breaks the cycle of violence. Why is there so little engagement and enthusiasm for trying out the possibilities and challenges the Christian faith puts before us? It seems to be time to re-examine some of our theological convictions and discover the fascinating potential there for new ways of action and reflection.

First of all we need a fresh look at **Christology**. Jesus died on the cross. Was that weakness? Or is it possible to interpret it – apart from all other theological dimensions – as an incredible strength, strength to carry to the ultimate a protest against a world without love of God and love of the neighbour, love of oneself and love of the enemy? God's son on the cross is perhaps the greatest challenge Christianity can bring to a world shaken by violence. A newborn baby as the Saviour of the world – could there be a stronger challenge than this belief to the world we experience? This dying man is our Lord. It is in him that we trust, not in the one with the sword who has the power to kill or to spare. Our Lord is the vulnerable newborn child and the rabbi and the man at the cross. Gil Bailie has written:

> The Johannine Jesus said that once he was raised up on the cross he would draw all humanity to himself, that gradually the sight of this innocent man on the gallows should become more compelling than all of conventional culture's techniques for making sanctioned violence morally respectable.[s2]

Christians must speak more about how Jesus lived and how Jesus died and the creative ways in which he opposed the powers in order to undermine the structures of sacred violence.

There is a need to look again at how we understand the **atonement**. What do we understand by original sin? Did God want the Son to die a violent death from the very beginning? Is Christ's death on the cross really necessary to save us? Did he have to die for our sins? A new emphasis on a trinitarian approach and recent discussions in the area of feminist theology might lead the way here.

Certainly a number of issues in the area of theological ethics must be considered anew. One of these has to do with the right and duty of **resistance** to evil, as we saw already in relation to Dietrich Bonhoeffer in chapter 2. This debate raises the question of the relation of the church to the nation and the state, as well as the **myth of redemptive violence**. Underlying all of this is the perennial issue of **power** and of structures that are violent in themselves and the basis for more violence. With **nationalism** and **ethnocentrism** on the rise, churches today are again tempted to identify with the nation in which they live. Thus the question of nationalism, which has been debated in the ecumenical movement since the WCC's founding, is still relevant. It should be one of the key insights gained in the century of the *oikoumene* that the one church of Jesus Christ is of no nation but that its unique character is precisely that it exists in all nations and is made up of people of all nations. A church identifying with a nation is a church which has gone astray and must be called back to its true identity by the community of churches.

We noted in chapter 1 that the secular world often expects religion to provide tools for dealing with the aftermath of violence. Christianity will have to find ways to speak about **forgiveness** and **reconciliation** as a precondition for breaking the cycle of violence in a way that the secular world can understand. Just as Bonhoeffer has explicated "cheap grace" as a distortion of the grace the Bible speaks about, so we must differentiate between the biblical concept of forgiveness and "cheap forgiveness". Forgiveness and reconciliation are extremely complex processes. As the German theologian Geiko Müller-Fahrenholz has suggested, they are an art, which must be discovered, taught and learned.[4] Forgiveness must face up to – and not try to ignore – just how difficult it is to live close to those who have done great violence to you. That applies to massacres just as much as to rape, to Rwanda just as much as to the Pacific. Talking about forgiveness in a world of violence must recognize that there is often an almost unbearable tension between the need to call for justice and the conviction that healing and wholeness of life require that we do not hate our enemies.

We will not always succeed in this process. As violence is the normal state of affairs which most people have grown up with and take for granted, there will be setbacks and shortfalls in any attempt to overcome it. Here the notion of **justification by faith** may be decisive in two respects: by enabling us to deal with failure, keeping those engaged strong enough to go on, and by helping us to overcome our traditional assumptions by reminding us that one is not worth less if one is weaker.

Witnessing – listening to the victims and remembering the martyrs – is an important Christian tradition. The church grows through testimony which links the stories of people to the story of Jesus. These stories must be told, must be made visible alongside the stories of domination and violence that prevail in the mass media. **Liberation** means that we read the story of the world with the eyes of those suffering from violence in the conviction that God is present precisely where people suffer violence.

Our faith allows us to challenge the basic assumption that there will always be violence. It offers us assurance that it is not naive to believe in overcoming violence. The Christian faith is a constant encouragement to believe in more than what we see; and the church must regain this **vision**: nothing is impossible – the resurrection of Christ is a proof of that. The theological debate must honestly face the objection that nonviolence ignores the fallen character of the world, the reality of sin. Any programme to overcome violence will have to clarify that it is aware that we live in a world where God's grace is present but which is not the new heaven and the new earth we are waiting for. Eschatology is future, but it has a present dimension. Thus the Programme to Overcome Violence should bring an eschatological vision to the consciousness of people. This is not a self-redemptive attitude. The question is whether Christians take the persistence of violence as a challenge to set footprints of how God wants the world to be or simply resign themselves to the way things are. About one-fifth of the population of the world identify themselves as Christians; they can make a difference if they consistently and credibly advocate nonviolence. They can help to create a new image of nonviolence as an active style of life, a sign of courage and the overcoming of fear.

As the traditional mechanisms of social cohesion and control seem to be collapsing, there is a growing interest in communal living and the moral resources for this. The churches' foundation of living in **community** should be brought into this debate. In our age of individualization people are coming to realize that the individual is not the answer but is often indeed at the root of violence.[4]

The Christian tradition has much to contribute to the understanding of a life in community of active nonviolence. Reflections in the ecumenical movement on the meaning of *koinonia* can be an important resource for this. But we cannot limit this to theological reflection and occasional public statements. Our conviction that the Word alone must be at the centre of Christian teaching must take into account that this Word became flesh, came to life in our midst. We cannot just watch and think and speak. We must also act, for we are accountable to one another and to God. Christians will always be called to resist the destruction of human life because it is the destruction of God who created us in God's image and who took on human flesh. It is time that the churches gain skills in nonviolent means as part of their practical theology. The struggle against violence needs to be an active struggle, for nonviolence is anything but passive.

Finally we have to take into account the rich resources **liturgy** provides, recognizing that it also grows out of the struggle. Examples of the latter include the "circles of silence" that came into being during the peace movement, silent protests with candles, the "Thursdays in Black" marked by women as a protest against rape and violence against women. What strengthens us, what keeps us going is that we can turn to God in prayer and song, in word and sacrament, and that we can turn to one another, being nourished by community in faith. Our worship together might help us to find new forms of responding to conflict.

Perhaps the recent programme of the WCC on Theology of Life will stimulate new ways of doing theology that can provide significant input into the Programme to Overcome Violence. We might discover an earth ethics that encourages us to become engaged for a new community living together nonviolently, creating space for life in justice and peace with respect for creation.[5]

* * *

The Programme to Overcome Violence is not just a matter of the church's practice but a deep challenge to theology. If the churches look anew at the basic themes of their theology, they will discover that they have a unique message to bring to the violence-ridden world they are part of: the notion of forgiveness, justification, healing and reconciliation. Offered in all humility, this may be a very valuable contribution to overcoming the dead-ends of secular society. At the same time, such reflection may lead to a renewal of Christian teaching and a rediscovery of the power of liturgy.

NOTES

[1.] A good overview, citing among others Jürgen Moltmann and Helmut Gollwitzer, is offered by Walter Kreck, *Grundfragen christlicher Ethik*, Munich, 1979, pp.332ff.
[2.] Gil Baillie, *Violence Unveiled*, New York, Crossroad, 1997, pp.227f.; cf. p.274.
[3.] See Geiko Müller-Fahrenholz, *The Art of Forgiveness*, Geneva, WCC, 1997.
[4.] On the relation between individualism and violence see Wilhelm Heitmeyer et al., eds, *Gewalt: Schattenseiten der Individualisierung bei Jugendlichen aus unterschiedlichen Milieus,* Weinheim and Munich, Juventa Verlag, *1995*.
[5.] See Larry Rasmussen, *Earth Community, Earth Ethics*, Maryknoll NY, Orbis, and Geneva, WCC, 1996.

7. Women, Youth and Children

A horrifying mass rape of schoolgirls took place at a residential college in Kenya in 1992. Several of the victims were even killed. When asked later why the staff had not come to rescue the girls, the headmistress said: "We did not think it was anything, only the boys raping the girls."

The weakest members of a community are the most vulnerable to violence; and in a time of rising violence it is women, youth and children who suffer the most. The Ecumenical Decade of Churches in Solidarity with Women has shown that violence against women is a reality across national, cultural and denominational boundaries. One of the most discouraging findings from the WCC's team visits to more than 300 churches around the world during the second half of the decade is that

> churches tend to let violent men go free and at the same time prevent women from speaking out against the violence. The failure of churches publicly to condemn such violence and state clearly that it is against the teachings of Christ appeared with distressing regularity.[1]

Evidence from many studies confirms the churches' reluctance to face this issue. Few church leaders see violence within the churches as a major question to theology, a threat to the very being of the church; and some male church leaders still legitimize it. Yet more and more Christians are coming to see that the churches are called to be at the forefront of the movement against violence against women.

The inability of churches to deal with violence against women is one of the clearest indicators of the urgency of a Programme to Overcome Violence for the churches. There is no way in which the churches can speak credibly about violence in society at large as long as they are not willing to deal with it inside church walls. Some quotations from the Decade report highlight that unwillingness:

- "One church leader spoke of 'disciplining' his wife and being thanked by her later."

- "Several others queried the definition of 'violence', wanting to distinguish between violence that resulted in death, and 'just hitting'."
- "Language that lowers the status of women continues to be used."
- "Many women are leaving churches because of what they experience as spiritual violence. They feel attacked by a 'violent theology' of 'God as demanding atonement' and 'violent images of salvation'."
- "The churches are responsible for the 'violence of silence'."

Because of their sex, women in all parts of the world daily become victims of specific human rights violations such as rape, whipping, circumcision, mutilation and murder. Most of the refugees in the world are women, many of whom have fled their homes to try to save the lives of their children. If they seek asylum in a so-called safe country, their gender again is an obstacle. Two examples from Germany, cited by Pro Asyl (Frankfurt) are typical. A single mother who recently fled Afghanistan was not granted asylum in Germany because the judge found that the rule of the Taliban according to which women are not allowed to have a job or to leave the home without being accompanied by a male does not constitute political persecution. In another case the rape of an Albanian woman by a policeman while she was handcuffed in a police car was not considered "relevant" to her request for asylum. Specific female reasons for flight are not recognized in German law. Violence in daily life is also accepted as normal for women who are citizens of so-called safe countries. As recently as September 1996 the Italian Supreme Court ruled that it is not a crime for a jealous man to beat his wife as long as he does not make a habit of it.[2]

Yet there are some signs of hope. The women in the war in the former Yugoslavia provided a great service to women all over the world by breaking the silence about the use of rape as a weapon of war. It is this growing readiness of women to speak openly about rape and battering that has made us aware that both are happening all over the world.

Women can no longer be silenced, and rapists cannot be confident that their victims will not speak out. Until the 1970s whatever happened within the family was seen as a private matter in France. But a civil movement of women succeeded in building up a whole system of women's shelters and offered legal and other forms of assistance to women. While 2459 penal reports about rape were registered in 1982, there were 7069 in 1995. Studies show that this does not indicate an increase in incidences of rape but in willingness to report it. Since 1990 rape in marriage in France is punished equally to rape of an unknown person.[3]

A story from Boston reports that clergy used to involve themselves in cases of wife battering only by trying to convince battered women to return to the husbands who had beaten them. A woman who reported battering by her husband was considered to be betraying her faith; and this judgment was often underlined with biblical quotations. Then in a training programme the pastors learned that the sanctity of marriage can be broken by violence as well as divorce. Many things have changed since then, slowly but successfully.

Other signs of hope that churches are starting to face violence against women within the church may also be mentioned. Education about it is taking place. From the pulpit both female and male pastors are beginning to speak about the reality of violence against women as a denial of the teachings of Jesus. Group discussions of women are being organized. Church groups are campaigning against sex tourism both in the countries of the North, where the "tourists" come from, and in the countries of the South, where women and children are dreadfully exploited in organized prostitution. Perhaps the most promising development is that men are starting to come together to reflect on what disposes them to violence against women. Recognizing this as a weakness they must overcome, they are developing training programmes.

All over the world violence is destroying the souls and lives of children. In most places the number of youth victims and youth offenders is growing. Again we must look first at structural violence: seven million children die every year of starvation and malnutrition – more than those who die of war, catastrophes or illness. Even in wealthy Germany, two-thirds of the growing number of people depending on social welfare are children. For the ecumenical movement, over-coming this violence means intensifying its critique of a global economic system that impoverishes a growing num-ber of people, especially children. It must examine the effects on children and youth of structural adjustment programmes of the International Monetary Fund, which insist on govern-ments cutting funds for schools and scholarships, while at the same time building up police and military forces.

When we look at violence against children we have to talk about child-battering and neglected children, street chil-dren, child prostitution, AIDS-infected children, children in war and forced conscription of children. Nor can churches treat this as a problem "out there": it is time to look closely at daily life in this context as well – at violence in the home, violence in school and the effects of violence in the media. Many churches which speak eloquently of the importance of the family scarcely mention these issues, although there is abundant evidence that a child who faces violence at home will be likely to use violence not only in rearing his or her own children but also in other relationships.

Education is a key element here. Many Christians still fall back on verses from Proverbs like "A wise child loves disci-pline" (13:1) or "Those who spare the rod hate their chil-dren" (13:24). It is much easier to force obedience by hitting or beating a child than to take the time to struggle for insight and compromise. But it is only in the latter way that the real authority of the parents can grow as mutual respect becomes the basis of the relationship. The churches should recognize parents' urgent need for advice in this area.

On the one hand, parents must be reminded that education is work. It needs effort and engagement. On the other hand, many parents today despair because they no longer know how to educate and they do not find values to hold on to. Author-ity and respect are dissolving, systems of value diminishing.

Christians would make an immense contribution by holding up nonviolent conflict resolution as something fundamental we must teach our children because it is at the heart of our faith. Churches might create groups in which parents could talk about their own daily struggle to overcome violence. Training programmes could be offered, using the wealth of available psychological and other resources on how to deal with one's own aggression. When parents fail in this daily struggle, the church could be a place to speak about it openly.

If churches are to be engaged effectively in this area they will have to face the fact that families today are no longer automatically a refuge. Because families have been idealized, the churches too often ignore the reality of domestic violence – psychological abuse, battering, neglect, rape. In order to be of any help, the churches will also have to accept the fact that many families no longer match the traditional constellation of mother, father and their children living in one household.

When I was a parish pastor and writing a regular column in a regional daily newspaper, the article that drew the most reaction was one I wrote about a day we were expecting visitors for dinner. I told how I tried to prepare a nice meal while one child was having problems with her homework, a second cut her finger, the baby needed her diaper changed and by the time I had dealt with all that, the fourth one had eaten all the salami off the pizza. I described how my anger and aggression had built up to the point that I was about to hit the children. But at the very last moment I found the energy to go to the garden, scream and slowly count to ten. After that I went back into the house and was actually able to laugh about the situation. Piles of letters arrived, in which mothers, fathers and grandparents shared stories of their own struggles and failures, feelings of guilt and perceptions of the "normality" of child battering. The volume of response brought home to me how urgent a topic this is and how little we in the church give advice or even talk about it. As Christians and churches we too often leave parents alone. In effect, because we do not develop a practical pedagogy about living and nonviolent dealing with conflict, we desert parents. How can children learn nonviolence if all they experience is that violence is the way?

There has been much debate in different sciences about whether "the inclination of the human heart is evil from youth", as the Bible puts it (Gen 8:20). Actually I cannot believe that God created human beings with an evil heart. What I see is that newborn babies first of all are helpless, longing for love and care. Already by the age of three, however, a change is apparent. There is a difference in behaviour, and aggression manifests itself. While we cannot here go into the old debate about "nature" and "nurture" – the relative roles of education and of inborn characteristics – it is obvious that the home has a fundamental part to play in education for violence or nonviolence. Where else but in the home can children learn that conflicts can be resolved in a nonviolent way, that giving in does not mean you are weaker, that compromise is necessary for living in community?

Again, we cannot individualize violence. Research shows that the more a family – whether a traditional family or a single-parent home – has to struggle with financial difficulties, the more likely violent behaviour is to erupt. Economic crisis brought on by unemployment or other factors is a major root cause of violence in the family.[4] In Munich, for example, the mistreatment of children has increased 54 percent since the economic situation in Germany began to decline.[5] In times of economic setback, church and society are challenged not to leave families alone. If this is true in a relatively wealthy society, how much more so in a situation where structural violence strikes children and those who care for them at a much more elementary level?

Schools are a second important factor in shaping the lives of children. Again reports from all over the world show that many schools today are a battleground. Violence among children and youth is a reality of the classroom and schoolground; and the structural conditions of school systems are inadequate or not flexible enough to react. While recent accounts of fatal shootings by children at schools in the US have drawn widespread attention to the "gun culture" and the ready availability of firearms, the phenomenon of violence in schools is not limited to that country. A study on violence in primary schools in Amsterdam in 1996 disclosed that 1200 of the 10- to 12-year old children – almost 10 percent – had hit a comrade so hard that he or she had to see a doctor. Forty percent of the primary school children admitted that they had threatened another child, 25 percent had done so with a stick or a knife and 2 percent had threatened a teacher with a weapon. Every third child had an experience of his or her belongings being destroyed by a fellow student. Forty percent of the children declared that they had taken part in a rumpus.[6]

The day after the Programme to Overcome Violence was introduced to the WCC Central Committee in 1996, the minister for cultural affairs in France called all schools in the country to have two hours of debate on violence in schools and conflict resolution. This is a sign of hope, because the usual reaction in many institutions and school administrators seems to be a tendency to hide the problem. But there are possibilities to change the situation. Experiments have shown that confrontation – a methodology coming from psychotherapy – may help to reintegrate aggressive children in school. A violent child who is confronted with his or her violence in a group of eight or nine may learn that it is "cool" to be able to deal with a conflict without violence. The fact is that many school children enjoy violence, because making victims is essential to their notion of life. Often, then, violent children and youth do not feel guilty but strong. Once they realize through confrontation that their status is at risk because their strategies of justification of violence are not accepted, they may start giving them up.[7]

Confrontation is by no means a cure-all. It is one of many methodologies that parents and teachers must be encouraged to try out, seeking advice from those trained in education for nonviolence. Parents, staff, pastors and other community representatives, even the children themselves can initiate round tables in order to place on the agenda a crisis which many schools would prefer to ignore. Rather than leaving schools and teachers alone with the problem of violence, we must encourage schools to take nonviolence up as a subject that needs to be taught.

Simple calls for stricter laws offer no solution. Jailing youth at a lower age and more consistently – the panacea which many demand – is not acceptable for Christians. We must take up the issue of prevention and the task of accompanying young delinquents. Passing rigid laws, opening new prisons, prohibiting youth to leave the home after 9:00 at night – all are signs of an inability to deal with the environment we put our young people into.[8] New and serious studies substantiate the link between violence and the individualization and structural and emotional disintegration of youth.[19]

Finally we cannot disregard the deep influence the media have on the attitudes of children and youth towards violence. The average 18-year-old in the countries of the North has spent 15,000 hours of his or her life in school, but 18,000 hours watching television.[10] In so doing they have witnessed 40,000 murders, rapes, shootings and other violent action. Animated cartoons and comics are especially violent. Someone is constantly being chased, bombed, killed. Moreover, nobody ever seems to learn anything: violence is the only way things happen.[11]

In the world of the mass media children and youth are recognized as consumers who influence the spending of billions of dollars every year. In advertisements aimed at children, traditional role patterns and violence play a decisive role. For instance, 35 million of the "virtual animal" Tamagotchi were sold through 1997. This plastic product "needs love and affection to survive" – an incredible perversion of images of human relationship. In December 1997 it was reported that "a brother" is being produced: DigiMon, a little digital monster that "needs the hard hand of a trainer to become big and strong in order to survive the hard battles of his life". The fighting mode can be activated by putting two monsters together. Apparently the new "toy" is aimed at boys aged 12 to 14.[12]

The stereotypes endure: Rambo never cries, Batman never fears, Lucky Luke never forgets to pull his gun. The invincibility of these violent heroes has a tremendous influence in shaping the way boys understand what it is to be male: being cool, aggressive, untouchable. Daring to show emotion or weakness means becoming the target of aggression of other boys. He-Man shows Barbie how to deal with life – an order that continues in the violent videos produced especially for young consumers. Children's books are not much different. The roles are fixed: fathers go to work, mothers stay at home. Girls have to be protected, boys are strong. Only rarely do children's books in Germany portray a father cooking or cleaning the house or a boy who is sad, fearful or crying.[13] Real men fight – the image of the strong and superior male pervades the media. That role image is decisive, and it is thus not surprising that statistics show that violence in the family and elsewhere is a predominantly male phenomenon.[14]

Churches can play a role in changing such stereotypes and thus contributing to overcoming violence only if they are ready first of all to change them within the church. That is not only a challenge to parish life but to theology as well. This will also mean changing some of our common vocabulary: for example, in the eyes of youth talking about a "war on drugs" gives legitimacy to the idea of resolving problems with violence.

In the introduction to a resource on domestic violence published by the Presbyterian Church in the USA, Thelma Burgonio Watson writes:

> Churches can be a resource to those who are the victims or the perpetrators of violence... Clergy and laity can learn the nature and causes of violence in the family and use the resources of our tradition appropriately to provide safety for victims, to stop the abuse by calling perpetrators to account, to restore relationships if possible and, if not, to mourn the loss of relationships.[15]

* * *

Violence strikes women, youth and children worst. The churches have a decisive role to play in supporting families, schools and street workers who are looking for new strategies. They can provide a place where parents and teachers speak openly about their failure and their daily struggle with violence. Churches can be the initiator of round tables, encouraging new methodologies. But in order to do so, the churches themselves will have to start to learn and practise nonviolence. The changing of role stereotypes of male and female is a decisive step in that direction.

NOTES

1 *Living Letters: A Report on Visits to the Churches During the Ecumenical Decade – Churches in Solidarity with Women*, Geneva, WCC, 1997, p.26. On violence against women see also Aruna Gnanadason, *No Longer a Secret: The Church and Violence Against Women*, rev. ed., Geneva, WCC, 1997, with its extensive list of resources from churches and related groups around the world, pp.85-105.

2 *The Times*, 18 Sept. 1996, p.12.

3 Cf. "Gewalt in den Familien", *Frankfurter Rundschau*, 31 May 1997, p.ZB5.

4 Cf. "Familie neu denken: Gespräch mit Sozialforscher Klaus Hurrelmann", *Evangelische Kommentare*, Sept. 1997, pp.516ff.

5 *Süddeutscher Zeitung*, 2-3 Nov. 1996, p.15.

6 *Evangelischer Pressedienst*, Zentralausgabe no. 193, 9 Oct. 1997, p.8.

7 "Gewalt bei Jugendlichen ist erlernt", *DLZ*, no. 3, 18 Jan. 1996, p.12.

8 On stiffer penalties as a panacea, see "Wie die Forderung nach härteren Strafen als Beruhigungspille dient", *Frankfurter Rundschau*, 9 Sept. 1997.

9 See Heitmeyer et al., *Gewalt: Schattenseiten der Individualisierung*, especially the interesting comparison of data from East and West Germany.

10 See Rainer Winkel, "Im Sog der Neuen Medien", in Margot Kaessmann, ed., *Medienkinder*, Hofgeismar, Evangelische Akademie, 1994. In the US, the average 18-year-old has logged 36,000 hours of television, according to Walter Wink, *Engaging the Powers*, p.23.

11 Wink, *ibid.*, p.18.

12 *Frankfurter Rundschau*, 16 Dec. 1997.

13 "Harte Jungs herrschen in Jugendbüchern", *Frankfurter Rundschau*, 19 Dec. 1997.

14 See "Tatort Familie", *Das Sonntagsblatt*, no.46, 15 Nov. 1996, p.16.

15 "New Resources on Domestic Violence", 5 Sept. 1997 (Internet).

8. Reflections on Complexity and Challenges

Against Violence

If one does not love the neighbour,
it is violence
If one does not teach the way
to a child who lost his way,
it is violence
If one does not give a cup of water
to a child who is thirsty,
it is violence
If one does not provide anything
to a hungry people,
it is violence
If one does allow violence of personality,
it is also violence![1]

As we have seen, attention to violence within the ecumenical movement has focused on the issues of war and peace, structural violence and, in recent years, violence against women; and a substantial body of literature exists on these three areas of concern.

But the subject of violence is far from exhausted by dealing with these questions. We must also address human rights violations: Amnesty International recently declared that there is torture in 120 states, that nonviolent political prisoners are in prison in more than 90 states and that people are subjected to political murder or disappearance in 70 states. Talking about violence also means talking about organized crime and terrorism, about gangs and drugs, about violence in the media and in sports, about education and nationalism. If we agree, as suggested earlier, that violence is a linking perspective on justice, peace and creation, ecological destruction must also be regarded as violence, and another large area of theory and action opens up. Furthermore, apart from the phenomenon of violence as such, there is a good deal of literature and research on the causes and constellations of violence, especially in medicine, psychology, sociology and philosophy, to be taken into account.

Indeed, violence is so broad a subject that it is tempting to deal separately with all these specific forms and facets of it. But the WCC's Programme to Overcome Violence dares a different approach: if violence is the ethos of our time, and if we see violence as an attack against God,[2] then churches should not let go of the insight that violence is a multi-faceted phenomenon which must be seen as a whole with its different dimensions understood as elements of one picture. The consequences of such an approach will have to be studied. Of course, the programme will have to find points of concentration like the Peace to the City campaign (see chapter 9). At the same time, its accent is on exploring possibilities for overcoming violence, not just listing the different expressions of the phenomenon. Furthermore, while war and peace remain a key concern, the programme will also bring to the surface experiences of violence in daily life, since it is obvious that concern is growing in churches all over the world about violence penetrating the everyday reality of people.

The ecological movement has often claimed that if the investment of human and financial resources which has gone into nuclear power plants had been devoted to the development of solar and wind energy, vast amounts of clean energy would be available by now. Similarly, one could argue that if humankind had put as much energy, creativity and experience into nonviolent ways of conflict resolution as into the development of weapons and preparations for war, the world would be a far safer place. For nonviolent conflict resolution is something which has to be learned and which is part of a process: if nonviolent methods are applied only at the last stage of a situation that has built up within the framework of violence, it will have great difficulties showing a positive outcome.

Nevertheless – astonishingly enough – it often does show results. Many examples can be found, many stories that are far too little known: the South African women being forced out of a squatter camp who stripped naked in front of the soldiers who, true to their good Dutch Reformed education, fled; or the old people on the island of Okinawa who began doing gymnastics every time the US Army prepared a training exercise for paratroopers at a certain place, obliging the US forces to call off the plans and give up training at that location; or the many cases of civil disobedience that use commercial strikes, boycotts or tax resistance to claim rights or land. Just as the red thread of nonviolent resistance can be traced within the Hebrew Bible (see chapter 4), so there is a growing history of nonviolent resistance in our days. We should discover it, make it known, draw lessons from it. The ecumenical movement can be a place where these stories are exchanged and the lessons are learned. Sharing these experiences could encourage Christians all over the world to learn and teach nonviolence as a means of resisting unjust structures and the destruction of creation and of conflict resolution.

Having acknowledged the complexity of the subject of violence, we must also raise the issue of definition. We may begin here with aggression, which is generally accepted to be an inborn force in human beings, related to the instinct of aggression in animals, which can develop in a constructive or a destructive way. One cannot overcome aggression, but it is possible to learn how to deal with it without hurting others. One could define violence as a specific form of aggression which intends to damage an object or a person.[3] This differentiates violence from force, which is not intentionally used to injure. Such a very first approach may be sufficient for the moment, though the matter of definition will have to come to play a more decisive role within the Programme to Overcome Violence.[4]

In this respect, the English-speaking community has an advantage over German-speakers, for example, since the German term *Gewalt* does not differentiate between power and violence. As there will always be aggression which tends to become violence, force will always be needed in order to counter it. This does not contradict the call to *overcome* violence: it is a matter of means and attitudes.

Having offered this provisional definition, however, we should also recognize that people's perceptions of violence may differ tremendously. For example, a survey in the 1970s showed that 57 percent of North American males believed that shooting a looter is not a violent act, while 22 percent regarded passive sit-ins as acts of violence.[5] These perceptions will of course differ from time to time, place to place, person to person; and an ecumenical address to the issue of violence must take these contextual variations into account.

At the same time, if we try to arrive at a definition of violence, nonviolence should be defined as well. One approach is to list the principles of nonviolence:
- respect for the opponent/everyone involved as fellow human beings;
- care for everyone involved in a conflict;
- refusal to harm, damage or degrade people/living things/the earth;
- if suffering is inevitable, willingness to take it on oneself rather than to inflict it on others; not retaliating to violence with violence;
- belief that everyone is capable of change;
- appeal to the opponents' "humanity";
- recognition that no one has a monopoly on truth, thus aiming to bring together our "truth" and the opponents' "truth";
- a belief that means are the ends-in-making, so the means have to be consistent with the ends;
- openness rather than secrecy.[6]

In countries where conscientious objection to military service is permitted, young men applying for this status are often asked what they would do if their girl-friend was being raped. Would they just stand by and watch? The point of course is to get the person to agree that it is necessary to defend oneself and others. But this reflects a fundamental misunderstanding of nonviolence, which equates it with defencelessness rather than recognizing it as a different methodology of defence. If we discover in the New Testament that Jesus teaches nonviolence and not nonresistance, a whole new perspective opens up. No one really knows beforehand how he or she will act in a situation of attack. But we can prepare for it.

The gun is not always the last resort. A gun may even be the first step in a chain of escalating violence. Or it may come not to be used at all, depending on the situation and the aggressor. Someone with a gun may be as helpless as someone who is unarmed. In situations of hostage-taking, a trained psychologist might be of more help than armed forces; and among police there is a growing awareness of the necessity to develop alternative methodologies to armed force.

Acknowledging the complexity of violence should not be an occasion of despair but a challenge to kindle creativity and to try to get hold of it from some new angle. One possibility is to look at the different forms in which violence appears, another is to look at the many methodologies developed to confront it, though the latter are almost as complex as violence itself. Without seeking to be in any way comprehensive, let us look in the remainder of this chapter at some examples of violence and methodologies for overcoming it as possibilities for churches to become active.

War remains the paradigm case of violence. It can be defined as a violent mass conflict in which two or more armies are involved and both sides show a minimum of central organization linked to a planned strategy.[7] This definition includes internal conflict, but does not apply to clashes between ethnic groups or gangs.

More than 50 wars and armed conflicts are going on in the world today, of which two-thirds are internal. Contrary to the perceptions of many in the North, the tendency to go to war is growing. Each year since 1945 there has been an average of about one war more than in the preceding year.[8]

A major change in war during this century has been in civilian deaths. In the first world war the ratio of soldiers killed to civilians killed was 20 to 1; in the second world war it was one soldier to five civilians, in the Vietnam war 1 to 13. In the 200 wars since 1945, 90 percent of all victims have been civilians – apart from the more than 33 million refugees.[9] Yet many Christians think there is little they can do about all this. But if every Christian in the world who is called to war would register as a conscientious objector, that would be quite an influential sign, especially because it would withdraw legitimation from war.

War is always an expression of failure to solve conflict by other means. In many parts of the world today centres are growing up for training in *prevention* and *mediation*. As a methodology for nonviolent peace-building, mediation begins from the assumption that in every conflict situation everyone has a perspective which is valid and needs to be understood. "Therefore, mediation is about enabling those in conflict to communicate with each other, to improve understandings and let truth grow."[10]

Given that the majority of conflicts today are internal (either against a regime in power or for greater autonomy of an ethnic group), the reasons for the conflict are quite well known. In many cases the combatants speak the same language. Thus centres for mediation seek to build up an "early warning system" to become active even before the different sides take up arms. An example of successful prevention is the severe tensions over the question of citizenship for Russians in Latvia and Estonia after the fall of the Soviet Union. The parties involved made use of international organizations to assist in finding a nonviolent way out of the conflict. While the conflict is not yet finally resolved, "conflict behaviour remained free of the use of direct violence. Attitudes have grown which allow to prepare for dialogue. Conflicting aims have been brought further into line with one another."[11] Even taking into account all its limitations, preventive diplomacy can work, but it requires a great deal of effort to make it work.

Not only preventive work is necessary, though. Post-conflict peace-building is a major thrust of United Nations policy. In July 1995 the UN Security Council decided to send 5500 Blue Helmets to Rwanda. It took five months for them to arrive; and when they finally did, their peacekeeping mission was outdated, since the civil war was over. What would have been needed then was support in reconstructing hospitals, schools and roads – but the Blue Helmets had no mandate for this.[12]

Within the framework of the WCC's conciliar process for Justice, Peace and the Integrity of Creation, a movement was initiated to create civil peace services or shalom-diaconates. This seems to be a promising concept: instead of training young people for war, they are taught peace-making and peace-keeping. Creative new ideas and structures for Christian and secular peace services are growing.[13] This is a great sign of hope, which could be linked to the experience of the "peace brigades" proposed by Mahatma Gandhi to the Indian National Congress in 1938 and organized from 1957 onwards.[14]

Two difficult questions regarding possible reactions to war at the international level remain unresolved. The first is whether intervention should be part of this concept. In recent years this question has arisen especially with regard to the Gulf war and the war in Bosnia. The peace movement in Europe was almost torn apart by the call for intervention from the victims on the one hand and by the conviction that nonviolence is the way to peace on the other. What must be reaffirmed is that after protracted violence, nonviolence cannot suddenly solve a conflict. A longer period of time is necessary, as well as acceptance of nonviolence as a means of conflict-resolution and training in those means.

The second question has to do with the effect of sanctions. While the WCC consistently supported economic sanctions against South Africa in the days of apartheid, there was strong sentiment within the Central Committee to reject the economic sanctions imposed against Serbia and Montenegro in the context of the violent breakup of the former Yugoslavia because of the suffering caused to the civilian population. An extensive memorandum on sanctions was received by the Central Committee in 1994, but the questions about the adequacy of sanctions as a nonviolent means still remain within the ecumenical movement.[15]

To break the cycle of violence it is important to deal with history. Often historical memories are able to create new violence generations and even centuries later. In the recent war in the former Yugoslavia, for example, one of the rallying points was the memory of Serbia's defeat by Turkish troops in the battle of Kosovo in 1389. To this day, that battle is interpreted as a symbol of the suffering of the Serbian people. What does it mean to carry a history like that for more than 600 years? Certainly it is important to remember our history, for if we lose our roots, we also lose an important part of our identity. On the other hand, we have to learn from our history if we are to avoid making the future into a repetition of the past and even worsening the situation. Who took what from whom and when, who committed injustices against a former generation – all this can easily lead to new violence and even war, if we do not see our history as something to learn from.

The only escape from such a cycle of violence is to face the truth and seek reconciliation. This has rarely been attempted at the national level – and that is why the Truth and Reconciliation Commission in South Africa is of special interest. Much has already been written about this unprecedented attempt to face history, to tell the stories and to reconcile in order to be able to build a future together. Truth has to be uncovered and has to be told. The recent work in the ecumenical movement on the question of impunity could also play a critical role in this context.[16]

Of special importance in this connection are schoolbooks. A fascinating December 1997 documentary televised in Germany explored how differently the very recent history of the Bosnian war is being taught in Bosnian, Croatian and Serbian schools. A major effort of truth and reconciliation is needed to tell the story from all sides – the rapes, killings and human rights violations by Croat, Bosnian and Serbian soldiers. Difficult and time-consuming though this may be, it is only if we heal the past that we shall be able to build the future. In the relationship between Germany and Poland, the work of a commission on schoolbooks has proved very valuable. If we have to tell the story with the eyes of the former enemy, we will tell it differently. Children will learn to see both sides of a conflict and recognize the position of one side as only part of truth.

Memorials can perhaps also contribute to making history part of a learning process. Ludwig Baumann, born on 13 December 1921, was forced into the German army at the age of 18. On 3 June 1942 he deserted, was caught and sentenced to death, but the execution was not carried out. Baumann survived and hoped for recognition he never received; instead, he was seen as a traitor.[17] To restore the dignity of those who refused to serve the destructive force of the *Wehrmacht* a movement has begun in Germany to create a memorial for those like Baumann who refused to go to war, the "deserters". The restoration of their dignity could be a meaningful way of helping young people to see that it is not orders but their conscience and responsibility before God which are the highest instance of personal decision-making.

An example from a completely different area is that of young prisoners. In New York, for instance, the crime rate has dropped significantly since the police forces have been increased – to one police officer for every 200 inhabitants. As a result, arrests have increased, and prisons are becoming more and more overcrowded.[18] A similar trend is seen in Germany, where there were more prisoners than ever before in 1996 – 48,900, or 23.8 percent more than in 1992, 96 percent of them men.

"Getting criminals off the street" is celebrated as a great success; but the story never ends with imprisonment. It is important to "unprime the life-long time bombs", says Jens Weidner, who has developed an anti-aggression training for violent offenders. The therapy Weidner has created trains especially young men in prisons to be able first of all to face what they have done from the aspect of the victim and then to restrain themselves from resorting to violence. Weidner does not start by analyzing but aims at different behaviour, so that young men leaving prison have a chance not to become repeat offenders.[19]

The mandate of the WCC's Programme to Overcome Violence puts the emphasis on "building a culture of peace through practical means to overcome violence at different levels of society and encouraging the churches to play a leading role in using nonviolent means such as prevention, mediation, intervention and education". This approach gives priority not to statements in reaction to instances of violence nor to the analysis of the phenomenon of violence, but to practical means to overcome violence. The option for nonviolence called for by the conciliar process for justice, peace and the integrity of creation becomes a pro-active concept. Churches should not wait until something happens and then react, but train pastors, parishioners and others in the skills of nonviolence and their application in the various areas of justice, peace and creation, at all levels from the international community to the personal life of the individual in the home and on the job. The fascinating insight is that people can be trained in the skills of nonviolence just as they can be trained in the skills of warfare. It is possible to *learn* nonviolence.

Equally important is the recognition that one *needs* training in order to be skilled in nonviolent action. Too often people seem to consider nonviolence as nothing more than a kind of pious hope – go and tell them to be peaceful – which is bound to fail because of human nature. But genuine and effective nonviolence requires qualifications. In the German city of Magdeburg, for instance, the church has provided a "peace pastor" who both mediates in conflict situations and trains others to be conflict counsellors, showing them how to moderate, counsel and mediate in situations of conflict. Police and community groups can then call on those counsellors when a conflict arises with a gang, for example. While some have raised questions about the appropriateness of the "shalom diaconate" suggested during the JPIC process, since it envisages training for mediators who go abroad, the Magdeburg example is one of training people in their own context to work in their own context. Similar examples can be found elsewhere in Germany. A police officer in Berlin specializes in training elderly women how to react if they are confronted with a purse-snatcher or someone attacks them in a tram. The programme has proved very successful. There is a similar training programme for the elderly in Cologne. "Prevention starts in the head," the trainer says.[20]

The philosopher Hannah Arendt has pointed out that even the toughest men in the Gestapo during the Nazi period were vulnerable when confronted with determined nonviolent resistance. For example, in March 1943 about 2000 Jews, mostly husbands and children of non-Jewish women, were taken into custody to be transported to Auschwitz. For five days women demonstrated in front of the building on the Rosenstrasse in Berlin where they were being held. When the SS set up machine guns, the women began to cry out: "Murderers! They are killing women and children!" The SS withdrew and on 6 March 1943 all the prisoners were released.[21] The nonviolent resistance was successful, the armed forces were helpless with regard to it. Regrettably, there are far too few stories like this from Nazi times, which makes it important to tell these because they counter the common assumption that nonviolence was of no use against the Nazis. Such stories – which can be found in very different times and contexts – exemplify that nonviolent resistance is not helpless, romantic and unrealistic. It can be practical and effective. We began by insisting that there is nothing romantic about violence; we should also add that there is nothing romantic about nonviolence either.

In 1997 the German public was shocked by reports of a 17-year-old girl who was raped on a tram. Despite her screams for help, nobody intervened, nobody went for assistance, indeed, several people got off the tram with the crying victim and the rapist still aboard. Nobody was ready to be a witness. We seem to have become a society of bystanders: ninety percent of people confronted with violence remain passive and silent, perhaps curious, perhaps indifferent; only ten percent would intervene.[22] In fact, if someone does dare to intervene, it is often quite effective: two days before this particular rape the same man had begun to molest two girls on the same tram, but when someone interfered he left.

We have to learn and teach civil courage again. While the culture of violence seems to be spreading, it is encouraging to see signs of a counter-movement of nonviolence as well. After the kidnapping of the 29-year-old Spanish politician

Miguel Angel Blanco by the Basque separatist movement ETA in 1997, more than one million people in Spain went into the streets to protest. Although Blanco was shot and killed, people from different regions in Spain had become united as never before against the terror, delegitimizing it. When ETA attacks claimed their 13th victim of the year in December 1997, people again went to the streets exclaiming, "Basques Yes, ETA No!" At least the ETA can no longer claim to be acting on behalf of the people.

Such stories need to be collected and remembered as sources of learning and encouragement. Nonviolence is an active concept. Nonviolence is not nonresistance. Nonviolence needs training. The churches are good places to tell and learn from these stories, just as the telling and retelling in daily life of the stories of Jesus is the basis of their faith.

In telling these stories a major challenge will be changing images and stereotypes and vocabulary. The philosopher Herbert Marcuse stated in the 1960s that breaking with the continuity of the ruling powers requires breaking with their vocabulary.[23] Popular culture especially feeds us with images of violence. Liberating ourselves and the younger generations from those images means making it clear that the real heroes, winners, champions are the persons who are able to renounce violence, who have the strength *not* to hit. This is a process of self-control as well as the effect of training. Only through empowerment of critical reason, self-knowledge, education and empathy can human beings learn to master their deeply rooted egoism and ethnocentrism, the irrational fear and readiness to hate that are sometimes more threatening than real weapons.[24]

The film *Antonia's World*, which won an Academy Award as the best foreign movie of 1996, has a sequence in which the granddaughter of the main character is raped as an act of revenge against the child's mother. The grandmother takes up a gun, goes to the pub where the rapist is celebrating his revenge and points the gun at him – but does not shoot. Trembling, she puts a spell on him that will haunt him for the rest of his life. This extremely intense scene, brilliantly portraying *not* pulling the trigger as an expression of strength, is a powerful testimony to the power of nonviolence.

Far more typical is the cinematic image of the fighting hero, though it was interesting to read recently that Sylvester Stallone, who played the part of Rambo, the main character in what was perhaps the most successful and most talked-about film of this type, said he now regrets having played the role. His experience of having an infant daughter go through open-heart surgery made him realize how precious and vulnerable life is. Perhaps the romanticizing of violence is no longer possible for those who have genuinely faced the vulnerability of life.

Since not everyone can be brought face-to-face with violence in order to overcome it, we must develop skills and methodologies to tell the stories not of the victor, but of the victim. For those who believe that the same Jesus who died on the cross is the Christ, the saviour of the world, that the baby in the manger in Bethlehem is the healer of the nations, there is already a firm foundation for telling the story of the victim. Christians need to rediscover our tradition on this point. The voice of the victims, the voice of the voiceless has to be made heard. Textbooks should not glorify military victories but convey the perspectives of those whose lives were destroyed in violent conflict. Their suffering should induce us to learn and teach nonviolent means of conflict resolution.

* * *

If the WCC's Programme to Overcome Violence wants churches to play a leading role in overcoming violence, they must be challenged to become centres of reflection and training for active nonviolence in their own context. The churches will have to give up being spectators of violence or merely lamenting it and become active within and outside the walls of the church. That demands courage, overcoming of fear, skills and creativity. In addition they will have to make room for listening to the stories of victims, so that the truth may be found in order to walk the path to reconciliation.

NOTES

[1] This poem by the Korean artist Hong Chong-Myung is published in Masao Takenaka, ed., *Christian Art in Asia*, Tokyo, Kyo Bun Kwan, 1975, p.168.

[2] Cf. W. Wink, *Engaging the Powers*, p.140.

[3] See Udo Rauchfleisch, *Allgegenwart von Gewalt*, Göttingen, Vandenhoeck and Ruprecht, 1992, p.36.

[4] See Peter W. Macky, *Violence: Right or Wrong?*, Word Books, 1973, pp.24ff.

[5] *Ibid.*, p.13.

[6] These principles are taken from "Overcoming Violence", a resource package from the Churches' Peace Forum of the Council of Churches for Britain and Ireland, London.

[7] Bernhard Moltmann, "Neue Gewaltmuster im internationalen Horizont", in K. von Bonin, ed., *Deutscher Evangelischer Kirchentag Hamburg 1995*, Gütersloh, 1995, p.488.

[8] Klaus Jürgen Gantzel, "Die Kriegsherde der Welt", in *Der Bürger im Staat*, Vol. 45, no. 1, 1995.

[9] Anton-Andreas Guah, "Zivilisierte Kriege", *Frankfurter Rundschau*, 13 Apr. 1995.

[10] Brendan McAllister, "Mediation within the Northern Ireland Conflict", unpublished paper for the REUNIR Conference, Biarritz-San Sebastian, 6-7 March 1997, p.3.

[11] Hanne-Margret Birckenbach, *Preventive Diplomacy through Fact-Finding*, Hamburg, Kieler Schriften zur Friedenswissenschaft, LIT Verlag, 1997, p.80.

[12] *Das Sonntagsblatt*, nr. 42, 17 Oct. 1997.

[13] See the report of the Council of the Evangelical Church in Germany, "Zukunft christlicher Friedensdienste", no. 12/1, for the synod of the EKD, Borkum, Nov. 1996.

[14] Christian Büttner, *Sechzig Jahre Friedensbrigaden: Schriften zur Gewaltfreiheit*, Lübeck, Gandhi Informationszentrum, 1993.

[15] *Minutes of the 46th Meeting of the WCC Central Committee*, Geneva, WCC, 1995, Appendix V, pp. 265ff.

[16] On the Truth and Reconciliation Commission see among others Geiko Müller Fahrenholz, *The Art of Forgiveness*, pp.83ff.; John de Gruchy, "Healing the Past for the Sake of the Future", in K. von Bonin, ed., *Deutscher Evangelischer Kirchentag Leipzig 1997*, Gütersloh, Gütersloher Verlagshaus, 1997, pp.616ff. On impunity, see Charles Harper, ed., *Impunity: An Ethical Perspective*, Geneva, WCC, 1996.

[17] Jörn Griesse, "Solange noch einige von uns leben", *Zivil*, Vol. 27, no.3, 1997, pp.24f.

[18] "Verfolgen, Verhaften, Einsperren", *Der Spiegel*, no. 29, 1997, pp.126ff.

[19] See Jens Weidner, *Anti-Agressivität-Training für Gewalttäter: ein deliktspezifisches Behandlungsangebot im Jugendvollzug*, Bonn, 1995.

70

[20] *Evangelischer Pressedienst* Nordrhein/Mittelrhein-Saar, no. 88, 1 Sept. 1997.
[21] Dietmar Böhm, "Die Macht der Gewaltfreiheit", *TAZ*, no. 3310, 19 Jan. 1991, p.16.
[22] *Die Zeit*, vol. 52, no.17, 18 Apr. 1997.
[23] Herbert Marcuse, *Versuch über die Befreiung*, Frankfurt, 1969, pp.43ff.
[24] Erik H. Erikson, *Kindheit und Gesellschaft*, Stuttgart, 1982, p.62.

9. The Seven-City Campaign

In July 1993 police in Rio de Janeiro killed eight street children. In August, 21 people were killed in a slum. As the number of violent attacks by street children on women and teenagers grew, a kind of panic broke out in the city. In September a group of people from very different sectors of society in Rio met to discuss what to do about the violence in their city. One idea was to campaign for two minutes of silence on a Friday at noon; and on 17 December that happened. The city stood still. The media, taxi drivers, even the stock market contributed two minutes of silence on this busy Friday just before Christmas – an impressive experience. Of course the silence did not eliminate violence. But it did raise awareness about violence in a new way, and created an idea of trust, solidarity and community on which future action against violence could build. Viva Rio was born.

The reference group convened to shape the WCC's Programme to Overcome Violence met in April 1996 in Rio de Janeiro to discuss what should be the initial focus of the programme, given the complexity of the issue and the risk that taking on too many of its facets at once could make it difficult to give the POV a profile. During the meeting the participants were increasingly struck by the fact that large cities are a microcosm of the world as a whole and of the many forms of violence in this world:

> They house the people and institutions that shape systems of globalization and national military rivalries. Cities demonstrate the global homogenization of norms, values and cultures represented in these systems. State and police violence are prominent in the city. Civil wars often take place in the midst of cities. Ethnic groups, youth and criminal elements use the city as a battleground. Women dare not venture out at night or during day in the wrong part of the city for fear of violence and rape, only to return home often to find no safety there either. Children, especially those in poor sections, have little safe room to play outside their homes and, like women, too often face the threat of beating and sexual abuse inside their homes.[1]

These characteristics are common around the world. Two out of three people living in big cities – three out of four in some parts of Africa and Latin America – have been victims of violence within the last five years. On the average, every fifth household in the big cities of the world has had a burglary during the last five years. In Uganda the figure is as high as 57 percent of the households.[2]

Facts and figures like this take on even greater significance from the rapid growth of cities all over the world. Habitat II, the UN summit on cities in May 1996, pointed to estimates that in the year 2005 half of the world's population will live in cities, ten years later there will be 23 metropolitan areas with more than 10 million inhabitants, seven with more than 20 million. Within 75 years the ratio between people living in rural areas and those living in cities will have totally reversed. Most of the four billion people living in cities in the year 2015 will belong to the poorest people of the world. According to an International Labour Office study, this poverty will lead to the collapse of the cities if there is not a rapid creation of infrastructure and jobs. If current trends continue, violence in the cities will only increase.[3]

The city is an important image in the Bible. This applies especially to the holy city of Jerusalem, but also to Babel, the city God destroyed to rebuke human pride (Gen. 11). The prophets use the image of the city in many ways. Isaiah in particular portrays the city as a sign of God's relationship with the people and the people's relationship with their God. The city is either faithful or becomes a whore (Isa. 1:21), the city can be exultant (23:7) or proud (23:9), God punishes the city (24:10), lays the lofty city low (26:5) and calls for rebuilding (45:13) so that Jerusalem will be called the City of the Lord (60:14). The rebuilding of the city is a symbol of the reconstruction of the covenant relationship between God and the people (Jer 30:18; 31:38). The city becomes part of the eschatological vision of the water of life, which flows through the middle of its streets (Rev. 22:2). That city will have no need of sun or moon, because the glory of God is its light and its lamp is the Lamb (Rev. 21:23). God will live in the holy city and will wipe away every tear; there will be no more mourning and crying and pain (Rev. 21.3f.).

Thus the city is both a microcosm of the world we experience and a symbol of our relationship with God and our eschatological vision of God's future, which will ultimately overcome the violence we face. The energy for all our efforts to overcome violence is the faith and knowledge that one day God will create true peace with justice and violence will be no more.

This is what lay behind the decision to focus the first campaign in the POV on the cities. Seven cities were chosen, in order to make the campaign manageable within the WCC's resources and to allow the cities to be in contact with one another. Care was taken to ensure a balance among the regions of the world. Of course, the number seven also has many familiar biblical resonances: God created the world in seven days, every seventh year is a sabbatical year and a jubilee year was to be proclaimed after seven cycles of seven years (Lev. 25), Jesus shared seven loaves of bread (Matt. 15:34), John wrote letters to seven parishes in the province of Asia Minor (Rev. 1:14).

But the campaign does not mean to limit the POV to seven cities; on the contrary, these cities are a point of departure for learning and sharing in which many can join in order to contribute from their own context and experience. Specifically, the Peace to the Cities campaign is supposed to highlight existing creative models of overcoming violence, of rebuilding community that has been destroyed, of building bridges between different communities. None of this action has been initiated by the WCC; its role is to publicize, encourage and link efforts for overcoming violence that are already underway in order to challenge churches all over the world to action of their own for building a culture of peace. It should be underscored that the decision to concentrate in the first phase on cities does not in any way mean that violence in rural areas is considered less important. The Programme to Overcome Violence provides a framework for many contexts to join. This campaign is a first focal point to introduce the programme and to highlight the issues.

The POV reference group thus looked for seven cities in which church groups – possibly in cooperation with others – are already engaged in overcoming violence. Rio de Janeiro, as noted above, was an obvious candidate. Though its image as a tropical paradise with glamorous beaches persists, during the past two decades it has faced a sharp increase in crime and violence. Estimates are that every year an average of 4000 people in Rio – 52 of every 100,000 inhabitants – die a violent death at the hands of their fellow citizens. The majority of those murdered come from the *favelas*, where they have already been victims of structural violence. And poverty in Rio is growing fast. One-third of the population of about five million (ten million in greater Rio) lives in one of 600 shanty towns. Only one-fifth of the households are linked to the city water system; and the sewage in the Bay of Rio, three-fourths of it coming from households,[4] makes evident how the structural violence which people suffer has consequences in violence against nature.

But Rio also offers a good example of cooperation between very different sectors of civil society, including the church. Viva Rio is a non-governmental organization that brings together representatives of these different sectors. Its goals are to reconcile a broken city, to bring back citizenship and solidarity in order to overcome social barriers and to fight fear and injustice. One of its strategies has been to try to re-establish a dialogue of trust between the police force and civil society. It has also created a voluntary civilian service as a mission for peace for 18-year-olds, as well as a nationwide campaign "Christmas without hunger, without violence".[5]

Since the POV had its cradle in South Africa, it seemed obvious to include a city there in the campaign, particularly since South Africa is one of the most violence-stricken countries of the world. In consultation with the South African Council of Churches Durban was chosen. Here the Diakonia Council of Churches is coordinating sixteen local organizations that are trying to break the cycle of violence in a part of South Africa that has suffered under severe ethnic clashes in the past. "When you entered the bar, we knew you had a gun and you were up to something. And when you started shooting, we were ready." This comment illustrates the state of relations in one area between members of the African National Congress (ANC) and the Inkatha Freedom Party (IFP), the two major political parties striving for political power. Violence between ANC and IFP supporters has plagued the province since the mid-1980s. Thousands have been killed in this violence. Between 1990, when Nelson Mandela was released from prison and the ban on the ANC was lifted, and 1996, when the first local government elections took place, more than 7600 lives were lost in the fighting in KwaZulu-Natal province and the Durban region. Nearly half a million people were displaced from their homes.

In Durban programmes on political dialogue and conflict resolution aim at drawing the attention of community members, political leaders and other civil society groups away from destructive forms of violence and towards constructive ways of approaching development issues in the region. Workshops targeting "no-go" areas empower participants with conflict resolution and mediation skills to enable them to mediate in a conflict before it becomes uncontrollable. Peace education also emphasizes the importance of peace and the value of political tolerance. Another important theme is stress and trauma healing for victims of violence.[6] Within the POV Durban could become a prime example of a city trying to build community by healing the wounds of the past so that peace declared becomes peace in daily reality.

Of several possible choices in North America, Boston was selected because of the creative efforts by three civil organizations which succeeded in reversing a trend of increasing violence, leading to a reduction in the murder rate by more than one-third within a two-year period. No one under 17 was killed by gun or knife between July 1995 and December 1997. The three organizations – the Boston Foundation Persistent Poverty Project, the Boston Coalition Against Drugs and Violence, and the Ten-Point Coalition –

focus on training programmes against domestic and family violence, street work with youths and community-building. This could become Boston's major contribution to the Peace to the Cities campaign. The Ten-Point Coalition, as noted in chapter 6, was created after a person was shot and literally died in a church. The congregation realized that they had to go to the streets in order to be the disciples of Christ. Several other pastors and congregations joined in order to take street violence as a priority. "We have to put our feet where our theology is," one of the pastors said.

In Europe, Belfast has become a symbol of violence linked to confessional differences – in this case between Protestants and Roman Catholics. Since "the troubles" in Northern Ireland began in 1969, more than 3000 people have been killed and 35,000 injured, tens of thousands have been bereaved, left unemployed or forced to move out of their homes. The Mediation Network for Northern Ireland in Belfast promotes the use of third-party intervention in disputes and supports creative responses to conflict in the community. It is trying to establish greater trust and respect between the segregated and divided people and encourages and supports churches in addressing the wider conflict in Ireland as an integral part of their ministry. Mediation is a central methodology for breaking the tradition of fear, prejudice and bigotry. Belfast could become a very good example of Christians and churches openly refusing to be identified as being at the centre of a conflict by recognizing the call to reconciliation as a step on the way towards nonviolence.

In Asia the decision was to focus on Colombo, where the National Peace Council of Sri Lanka (NPC) grew out of a campaign against election violence in July 1994. An interreligious group of organizations and individuals joined to create a wall poster campaign and later convened a peace conference. In opposition to government rhetoric about "war for peace", the NPC insists that the war between Sinhalese and Tamils can be ended only by negotiations. Here Christians might play an important role, since the members of the Christian churches come from both ethnic groups. The NPC is engaged in negotiation, community-building, refugee assistance and capacity-building among parliamentarians.

In addition, the National Peace Delegates Convention has formed a steering committee drawn from more than thirty organizations which attended the initial meeting and fixed a date for a national peace convention in connection with celebrations of the 50th anniversary of Sri Lanka's independence. The convention will provide an opportunity for the voiceless victims of the "hidden war" to tell their story to the world. Colombo could illuminate, amidst a conflict that mixes ethnic and religious motives, the possibility to rediscover traditional methods by which different groups can live together peacefully in society.

The remaining two cities come from island regions of the world: the Caribbean and the Pacific. In Kingston, Jamaica, the issue of children and youth may be highlighted, because Kingston has a high proportion of juvenile crime. Suva, Fiji, must deal with tensions between respecting the rights of indigenous Fijians and accommodating the desire for equality of Indo-Fijians.

There are many stories to be told about the seven cities involved in the campaign. Some of them will be included in a book to be published later in 1998. But newer media are also being fully used. Each city is producing a video to tell its story. Out of this a common video will be produced. Moreover the Internet is serving as a point of information and debate for the campaign. Each city posts a newsletter on the WCC's WorldWideWeb site (http://wcc-coe.org/pov) every month to give latest information. From time to time a chat is organized for purposes of exchange, counsel and encouragement. Others can comment and bring in new ideas. The first results of this experiment have been very promising. In effect, the programme is using the media – which are so often a factor in supporting and even glorifying violence – as a means to counter violence.

One of the most significant similarities of the stories from the seven cities is the tremendous changes that can result when people from different parties in a conflict are brought together: the building of trust, the possibility of seeing the conflict through the eyes of the other. But although this and other elements of the methodology of mediation seem applicable in various ways in many places, most people in the churches do not know about it. They are not trained to become the experts in conflict resolution which one might expect from those who confess the name of the Prince of Peace. The exchange of methodologies and stories, of failures and successes could encourage others to leave the position of the spectator. The experience several cities have with interfaith cooperation will probably become a very important aspect. As Donna Parchment from Kingston has said, "It is already a step forward for us to learn that we are not the only ones facing these problems!"

The different focal points of the engagement against violence in the seven cities could bring about a learning process for the others. For instance, Belfast and Colombo are dealing with ethnic or sectarian conflict, Boston and Rio are dealing mainly with street violence. Some of the contexts clearly show interfaith dimensions, others take up the issue of racism, others show new possibilities of action across class barriers because the conflicts are beyond class (Rio). Similarities are already emerging; for example, there seems to be a new perspective on cooperation between civil society and government, rather than automatically seeing society against government. In many cities the police are becoming a factor of cooperation. The distinction between social and political violence is becoming important. With interfaith relations a challenging factor in most cities, it is possible to see a great promise of renewal if religion were to become a bridge to peace instead of a factor of separation and violence.

* * *

Within the Programme to Overcome Violence, the Peace to the City campaign is a very good pointer to the fact that peace does not come from above. It has to grow at grassroots level and be nurtured by the creativity of the people. The churches should become engaged at that very level because this is where they also exist. The linkages which the ecumenical movement provides between different contexts can facilitate the networking that is necessary to share and learn across contexts. Especially the challenge to cooperate locally with civil society at large and to engage in interreligious dialogue may gain insight and encouragement from reflection and exchange at international level.

NOTES

[1] *Overcoming Violence*, Geneva, WCC, 1997, p.35.
[2] *Evangelischer Pressedienst*, Zentralausgabe no. 163, 27 Aug. 1997.
[3] *Ibid.*, Dritte Welt no. 100, 19 May 1996.
[4] *Ibid.*, Dritte Welt no. 102, 31 May 1996.
[5] These data are taken from the Viva Rio newsletter no. 1, Dec. 1997.
[6] From POV Durban bulletin no. 1 (Internet).

10. Perspectives for the Future

A small room off the entrance to some old churches in Norway is called "the weapon house". Here worshippers were supposed to take off their weapons before going into the house of the Lord. A quaint throwback to an earlier era? Not quite. Ecumenical News International *reported recently: "Citizens of the US state of Texas who have a licence to carry a concealed weapon can take their pistols into churches, unless there is a sign on the church door forbidding it."* [1]

Two areas have been suggested in which the Programme to Overcome Violence could sharpen perceptions within the ecumenical movement: the challenge of small arms and community policing.

Arms production and the arms trade have long been on the agenda of the ecumenical movement. For much of the cold war, the focus was on nuclear disarmament. But the end of the cold war has by no means broken the cycle. Turkey for instance plans to buy weapons worth US$50 billion within the next 25 years, apparently selecting vendors according to a "red list" which ensures that arms manufacturers in countries which criticize Turkey's human rights record do not get orders. Examples of how economic interests and the nonviolent movement might conflict are evident. Germany, for example, decided in 1997 to buy 180 military Eurofighter planes for more than DM23 billion – mostly, it was said, to save jobs in the weapons industry – while at the same time the government was making severe cuts in social welfare programmes.

But a new "agenda from below" which the Programme to Overcome Violence might address is the issue of small arms or light weapons. This concern emerges from all of the cities in the Peace to the City Campaign as well as many other places. After the shock of the tragedy in Dunblane, Scotland, in 1996, when a man killed young school children and one of their teachers, the families of the victims began a successful campaign against handguns, which culminated in June 1997 with passage in the House of Commons, by an overwhelming majority, of a firearms bill which extended an earlier ban on large-calibre handguns, thereby outlawing all privately owned handguns in Great Britain and Northern Ireland. This was a positive and encouraging development for people around the United Kingdom whose safety is threatened by these weapons. But why was a massacre necessary to start the campaign? Why was it limited to Britain? The threat which small arms pose to individuals and communities and the climate of violence which is created by their very presence, is an issue all over the world. There is nothing normal about carrying around a handgun, and there is no apparent reason why it should be considered one's right to do so.

If the churches are to take up this issue they will have to make linkages with secular movements. A recent example of the potential effectiveness of international coalitions of this type is the landmines campaign, which could be seen as another facet of what might be called micro-disarmament. More than 110 million landmines lie unexploded in former war zones. Twenty thousand people are killed by landmines every year, tens of thousands are crippled. When one considers what the armaments industry earns by the production of mines, the link between economy and violence again becomes obvious. When an international convention against anti-personnel mines became a reality in December 1997 – even though the US and China have refused to sign it – this was possible only because of a wide-ranging coalition. The signing of this treaty is of course only a first step; and it will take many years of expensive work to clear the mines already in place around the world. However, the signing of the convention and the awarding of the 1997 Nobel Peace Price to the International Campaign for the Prohibition of Landmines was a notable step forward. Jody Williams, the coordinator of the campaign, said in Oslo during the Nobel ceremony on 10 December 1997: "For the first time the states had to respond to the will of civil society and had to sign a treaty that expresses that will."

The churches could play a leading role in coalition-building around the issue of small arms. They are in a position to call together civil society organizations in order to involve local activists and those who are politically involved as well as grassroots supporters. Or they could become part of coalitions brought into being by others. The role of light weapons within society as well as in intra-state conflicts must be analyzed. Such an analysis must be linked to the profits earned by the manufacturers of light weapons – companies living in the same communities as the churches and often employing their members. Dialogue is necessary. Is a nonviolence movement really a threat to the economy? Both the methodology of mediation and the methodology of networking will be useful in confronting this issue.

In all seven of the cities in the campaign, questions about policing have surfaced. Are the police seen as "the other", chronic violators of human rights, or are they a necessary force to resist violence? Is it possible to communicate with the police, to integrate them into efforts to overcome violence within the community? The insights coming out of the Peace to the City campaign can be linked with experiences in other contexts. For example, interesting projects of cooperation have been initiated between civil society groups and police in Paris and Berlin.[2] Community policing is an issue that churches and local congregations could take up around the world.

Besides these two specific focal points, it is clear that many other facets of the reality of violence would be identified as points of engagement for the churches. Fundamental is the local level, as we have seen, as congregations, parishes and community groups respond together to their local experiences of violence. At the national and regional levels, churches can also initiate or join campaigns that are relevant to their specific context. Albert Einstein once wrote that the realization of the aims of pacifism could happen only through a supra-national organization.[3] What he said about ending the use of armed conflict in relations between states can be applied more generally to overcoming violence in all its dimensions. Thus the World Council of Churches has a broad range of possibilities for making a valuable contribution to local, national and regional initiatives to overcome violence:

- The WCC has often been a *story-telling* community. Because violence and nonviolence are not abstract categories but always have human faces, there are many stories of overcoming violence to be told. Stories of violence are of course widely reported, as our random survey in chapter 1 of one day's newspaper made evident. The challenge is rather to write the history that seldom hits the front pages, in order to encourage others. As the stories of overcoming violence are collected from all over the world, a new picture will take shape: we are living in a violent world, but there is an alternative reality all over the world as well. By linking the stories of successful mediation and imaginative action, the WCC can bring nonviolence to the surface as an active form of witnessing to the Christian faith. The Council and the Programme to Overcome Violence can serve as a clearing house and switchboard.
- Through the POV the Council can open up new avenues for *dialogue*. It is significant that in many local communities evangelical churches which have not been involved in conventional ecumenical bodies are active partners in the struggle against violence. New dimensions of ecumenical cooperation could open up with the Roman Catholic Church. Such openness to dialogue applies also in regard to other faiths. The local experiences in the Peace to the City campaign – in Boston with the Jewish community, in Colombo with the Buddhist community, for example – could be considerably supported and strengthened by international interreligious dialogue about nonviolence and violence. If the religions of the world would join in rejecting violence, the all-too-frequent misuse of religion to fuel conflict could be successfully countered.
- We have pointed earlier to the need for intensified analysis, research and debate in the *theological* area. In addition, if the churches are to play a leading role in using nonviolent means, practical theology will have to take up the question of the skills and training that are necessary

for mediation. Clergy and lay people in the church have to be trained in order to make the voice of the churches credible. Peace requires more than the desire for it; the will to peace is not enough. But having a few trained specialists in nonviolent conflict resolution is not enough either: there has to be an impact on the teaching and preaching of the church. While these challenges need to take effect at the grassroots level, they can be encouraged by the WCC.

- *Campaigns* at the international level, relating to the United Nations and its agencies as well as a range of other intergovernmental and nongovernmental organizations, should be supported by the ecumenical movement internationally, including the WCC.
- At the same time, the WCC will have to challenge its *member churches* to witness to the peace of Christ and not to fall into the traps of identification with ethnic pride, national goals, wars.
- The WCC can draw on its own rich experience in linking *action and reflection*. Within the structures of the Council itself that means continuously identifying the linkages between the Programme to Overcome Violence and the many other activities and concerns on the agenda. This will bring both new insights and perspectives into the engagement against violence and new networks and constituencies to join the struggle.
- One of the major contributions of the ecumenical movement could be opening a *perspective beyond conflict*. Commitments and efforts to overcome violence must be sustained by the glimpse of something new that is possible. The vision of living together as brothers and sisters which is promised to us in the Bible, as well as the foretaste of that community we have in daily life and in the eucharist, must be celebrated. Certainly our liturgies must make room for lamentation regarding the reality of violence and mourning its victims. But this cannot be the last word. They must also be full of hope and celebration

when it comes to God's promised future and the counter-reality we already experience.

Perhaps one of the most significant elements the churches can contribute to overcoming violence is the belief that people can change. They can change as did Saul, who once "breathed threats and murder against the disciples of the Lord" (Acts 9:1), when he became Paul the apostle. They can change like Billy Mitchell and Liam Maskey in Northern Ireland, former members of the Irish Republican Army (IRA) who are now promoting peace. Churches can testify to and contribute to the hope that one day God's justice will overcome all our differences, that justice and peace will embrace one another, truth and righteousness will prevail (Ps. 85:10). Until that day we are called to do our best to set up signs of that knowledge in a world of violence and injustice. We can be encouraged to leave our safe havens, go out into a violent world in solidarity with the people and work for a world where life is safe for all, especially the most vulnerable.

In setting up the Programme to Overcome Violence, the WCC did not suppose that it would do away with violence once and forever. Those engaged are not romantic: they see the challenge of violence as a challenge to the good news, and they expect to confront backlash, indifference and failures. For instance the execution by the military regime in Nigeria in 1996 of Ken Saro Wiwa and several of his comrades who had nonviolently struggled for the rights of the Ogoni people and against the destruction of their land was difficult to bear, as are all such setbacks. But Christians also acknowledge that now we only know in part, but when the complete comes, the partial will come to an end (1 Cor. 13:9f.). We have to point out though that conflicts are not really solved by violence either; instead, they

> fester to become the source of later conflicts and even long-standing animosities. Conversely, when mediated solutions are owned by both sides, peace is more stable and enduring... Though nonviolence will not always work, history is full of failed attempts to establish lasting peace by using force.[4]

The chain of violence obviously cannot be broken by violence – the challenge is to dare nonviolence. The gospel gives Christians the support they need not to fear failure and the hope and vision they need to avoid resignation. "Neither exaltation of power nor the search for vengeance will ever solve any human situation. In accepting death, Jesus showed us the only possible way."[5]

What the Programme to Overcome Violence could bring to the ecumenical movement is a change of perspective: instead of staring at violence and lamenting it, we can make nonviolent action as the point of reference. A whole new movement could originate from that.

* * *

The POV is full of challenges yet to be discovered. It faces enormous complexities and is confronted with many open questions. Nevertheless we can see small but promising beginnings and we can identify some potential next steps in the themes of light weapons and community policing. Many more possibilities may be found; and ecumenically the WCC can play a decisive and exciting role in uncovering these. It will depend on the churches regionally and locally to take up the chance offered by this programme to witness to the gospel in a world of violence. While aggression and violence will be with us until God's future comes, nonviolence is the path to walk for the disciples of Christ.

NOTES

[1] *Ecumenical News International Bulletin*, no.22, 12 Nov. 1997, p.9.
[2] "Nichts als reden, reden, reden: In der Pariser Vororten bekämpft die Polizei Gewalt, indem sie das Vertrauen Jugendlicher zu gewinnen sucht", *Frankfurter Rundschau*, 19 Dec. 1997; Dorothee Beck, "Gehört Gewalt zum männlichen Verhaltensrepertoire'?", *ibid.*, 15 March 1997.
[3] Albert Einstein, *Ueber den Frieden: Weltordnung oder Weltuntergang?*, Bern, 1975, p.561.
[4] Paul Anderson, "Jesus and Peace", *loc. cit.*, p.125.
[5] Jacques Ellul, *Violence*, p.174.